Memoirs Of A Deist

J. Hatchard And Son Publisher

MEMOIRS

OF

A DEIST,

WRITTEN FIRST A. D. 1793—4;

BEING A NARRATIVE OF THE

LIFE AND OPINIONS OF THE WRITER,

UNTIL THE PERIOD OF HIS CONVERSION TO THE FAITH OF

JESUS CHRIST;

WHICH TOOK PLACE IN THE COURSE OF THE DEVELOPMENTS

OF AN ESSAY, WRITTEN BY THE DEIST,

TO PROVE THAT

PURE DEISM WAS THE ONLY TRUE RELIGION.

" No man, when he hath lighted a candle, covereth it with a vessel, or
" putteth it under a bed; but setteth it on a candlestick, that they
" which enter in may see the light."—LUKE, viii. 16.

" Come and hear all ye that fear GOD, and I will declare what HE hath
" done for my soul.—PSALM lxvi.

LONDON:

PRINTED FOR

J. HATCHARD AND SON, 187, PICCADILLY.

1824.

131

PREFACE.

In lieu of a formal Preface of my own composition, I venture to prefix to the following pages, an extract from a letter to the Author, written by the Rev. John Newton, late Rector of St. Mary's Woolnoth, on the subject of this Narrative. For after writing several Prefaces, it appeared to me, that the above-mentioned extract contained, in few words, nearly all that was necessary for the Reader's information; and that the opinion of a second person respecting my work, would have more weight than my own.

I shall only just observe here, that my first Preface (written when I was as it were red hot with zeal and faith, without judgment) was a burst of enthusiasm*; containing, *perhaps*, some striking and useful observations, but in general hardly intelligible to any one except myself, and what would be thought rank and mystical fanaticism. This piece was successively weeded and moderated by different criticisms, until it *perhaps* contained nothing offensive except the

---

.* In a common and general sense, not meaning a bad sense.

insipidity of tedious common place, as many might probably have thought it.

This residuum, as uninteresting, and perhaps repulsive, I at last burnt; and finding upon the whole, that I could not hope to please more than a very few of my Readers, on any terms, I began to think that it would be better to have no Preface. But when I recollected Mr. Newton's Letter on the same subject, it struck me that an extract from it would form the best Preface which I could prefix to the work. Probably some persons may say, we are already overwhelmed with these Narratives; why publish it at all? I reply, that after keeping it near *thirty years* in my trunk, I am now induced to publish it, by the earnest solicitation of some pious friends.

It appears necessary, in self-defence, to inform my candid Reader, that when I first wrote this Narrative, I was, perhaps, one of the most romantic simpletons in existence. I had it in my most deliberate purpose, to exhibit my whole soul for public inspection, like an anatomical subject, *pro bono publico*, as a warning to sinners, and also as a valuable study for spiritual anatomists. At the same time, I intended to remain incognito, if possible, without defeating the object of publication. For I was a bachelor, a soldier, and an enthusiast; I therefore committed to paper every thing

that I knew or thought of myself, both good
and bad, in thought and word, as well as
in deed; that the whole naked truth might appear, for the information of my moral and
spiritual dissectors, and ultimately for the glory
of God, in the confirmation of the truth of the
Gospel.

One half, to say the least, of these exposures
of myself, has been expunged by the advice of
the Rev. Mr. Newton, who anxiously desired to
revise, and curtail with his own hand, and then
publish the corrected Narrative. But at that
time my prejudices were too inveterate, and my
attachment to some parts which he desired to
cut off too *parental*, to allow me to consent to
his proposed operations, which I thought too
severe, too concise!

At present I find that there is scarcely a
part in the whole, which does not displease
some one or other of even those who wish to
see the MSS. in print. If, therefore, I would
please the whole, I must expunge the whole;
and consequently I resolve to let it go as it now
stands. Yet, I hope that I do really desire to
" *please my neighbour for his good to edifica-*
" *tion.*"—1 Cor. xv.

Extract from Mr. Newton's Letter to the
Author.

" I have now read your book twice, with
" some attention: the greater part of it with

" pleasure and admiration. Though I have rea-
" son enough to distrust my own judgment,"
(yet) " I hope I am not deceived myself, and
" therefore shall not mislead you if you follow
" my advice."

" Excepting what I have excepted, I think
" your book will be one of the most important,
" and if the Lord pleases to give his blessing,
" may be one of the most useful publications
" of the age (1800). I know no book that
" displays such an exhibition of the heart of
" man, or (scarcely excepting my own Narra-
" tive) such an instance of the wonderful rich
" grace of the mercy of God to a chief sinner.
" Your reflections also are in general solid, judi-
" cious, striking, and pertinent; perhaps here
" and there, some of them are rather tinctured
" by your lively imagination. But I have chiefly
" confined my objections to those things which
" would be thought indecent, especially in this
" refined and sentimental age. Some regard
" is due to times and circumstances, &c. I am,
" dear Sir, your affectionate J. N. 12th Nov.
" 1796."

I would add, that in consequence of Mr.
Newton's advice, this Narrative has been weeded; or, changing the figure, I may say hewed,
so as scarcely to contain one half of the original
mass. It also may be proper to say, that the
Author is an illiterate soldier, whose Greek

does not extend beyond the New Testament, nor his Latin beyond the common school-books now forgotten. Hence my Reader must not expect to find an eloquent captivating style. In short, perspicuity and fidelity are the chief objects aimed at in this imperfect sketch.

Lastly, I beg to assure my Reader, that (as I am not in any pecuniary distress, nor in straightened circumstances) if any profit should arise from the sale of this work (a most improbable event, no doubt!) it will be devoted as a mite to missionary purposes.

N. B. I cannot resist the temptation of lengthening my Preface a little, by an extract from the Quarterly Review of July, 1822, No. LIII. page 136; which has just met my eye; and which seems well adapted to mollify prejudices against certain novelties, that will be found in the course of the following Narrative; viz.

" All error on moral or political subjects
" is in itself mischievous; but such is their
" difficulty, that no work, of any length, on any
" of those subjects, was ever free from error; or, if
" it had been free, would have been thought so,
" by those, whose prejudices it contradicted. In
" proportion to the originality of the work, will
" its apparent and its real errors be multiplied.
" It will oppose more received opinions, and
" its conclusions will want the qualifications of

" which further discussion will prove the ne-
" cessity ; and in proportion to the practical
" importance of its topics, will the injurious
" tendency of its errors be more glaring. In
" every original work, therefore, on an im-
" portant moral or political subject, a judge
" must find passages, which he thinks mischie-
" vous; or (which is enough for the rule) of
" which he is not sure that the tendency may
" not be mischievous. In proportion to its
" originality and importance, it must be sus-
" ceptible of this literary outlawry.   We will
" not waste the time, or insult the understand-
" ing of our Readers, by proving the utility of
" such works, or by showing that even the
" discussion of their errors leads to truths,
" which *might not*, probably *would not*, other-
" wise have been attained."

MEMOIRS,

&c.

PART THE FIRST.

" Hé that soweth the *good seed* is *the Son of Man*.
" *The field* is *the world*. The good seed are the
" children of the kingdom; but *the tares* are the
" children of *the wicked one* : the enemy that sowed
" them is the devil."—Matt. xiii.

As it is natural that my readers should wish
to know something of the person whose narrative they are about to peruse, and whose name
they may perhaps discover, I shall endeavour
to oblige them by telling all I know. Indeed
more than I actually know; for I only *understand* that my ancestors (I must have had ancestors) were originally from France. They
were probably Hugonots, who settled first in the
Island of Jersey or Guernsey, and afterwards
in England and in Ireland. My father was a
sailor, a lieutenant, originally in the navy, and
afterwards commanded one of the government
packets to Lisbon. My mother was the daughter of an English merchant at that place ; and

I *understand* from my only living relation, my
sister (four or five years older than myself),
that my grandmother insisted on my father's
leaving the navy and getting a Lisbon packet,
before she would consent to give him her favourite daughter.

My parents both died during my infancy,
or nearly so: that is to say, my father when I
was four, and my mother when I was six years
of age. Of the first I remember but little, except that he once flogged me for telling a lie,
and that he probably made me a soldier, at least
instrumentally, by giving me drums, swords,
caps, and colours. My mother was a woman of
retired piety and meekness; and I remember
that she made me learn several of Watts's
Hymns and some Psalms by heart, among
which I particularly recollect the 139th.

My guardian, who was also my uncle by
marriage, was in the East India Company's
civil service at China, and upon the whole a
very worthy man. He was strictly honest, and
very attentive to religious duties of an external
nature; but his temper and his tongue were
not always so well regulated as they should
have been: not that he ever swore, but he was
morose, severe, and, as I thought, rather inclined to tyrannise, where he had power.

The first school to which I was sent, at about
seven years of age, in 1764, was, in respect to

moral and religious considerations, extremely dangerous. The master was a proverbial miser, and probably consulted nothing beyond œconomy in all his arrangements. Thence it happened, that boys of all ages, and even young men, were indiscriminately mingled together, not only in the play-ground but also in their bed-rooms, which I soon perceived to be a most execrable custom.

At or about the age of nine years, I was providentially taken from this place, and was sent to a very reputable school at Greenwich, kept by the Rev. Doctor B. where considerable care was taken, speaking of those times, 1768, to preserve the morals, and cultivate the minds of the scholars; so that had I not laboured under certain peculiar disadvantages, I might have made a tolerable progress in school knowledge.

The little advance which I made in my studies originated from the following singular cause. At the first school to which I was sent, a fit of rage which transported me one day, in a quarrel with another boy, and for which I ought to have been flogged, was mistaken, first by an old woman, to show her sagacity; next by an apothecary, to dispose of his drugs perhaps; and lastly by every one else, on the authority of the two first, for a fit of real insanity. In consequence of this opinion (in which I rea-

dily acquiesced, as it gained me a great number
of play-days, and a vast fund of amusement, in
alarming and pursuing those who feared to be
bit by me), I was taken from school, and
issued, physicked, and sea-bathed during two
years, until I began really to believe it myself.

When I was afterwards placed under Doctor
B. my uncommon case was explained to him,
and he was particularly desired never to flog
me, or even to frighten me, if it could be
avoided. Being permitted to choose what I
would learn, I declined altogether to meddle
with Greek, which alarmed me by its name
and unknown character; and with respect to
my Latin I was extremely idle and careless.
Thus my imposture was punished by the loss of
all the advantages which I should have derived
from the knowledge of the Greek language, and
which I now know to be great, though I have
lately (eight months of 1819) learned to read
the Greek Testament by the aid of a lexicon.

Yet to those parts of education which are
enlivened by the glowing colours that spring
from the imagination and heart, I was neither
insensible nor indifferent; and though I forfeited the greatest part of my weekly allowances
for lying abed during the morning school, yet
the pleasure that I took in drawing, often roused
me at four o'clock in the morning, in winter,
to work at a favourite design, even by candle-

light. French, the use of the globes, fortification, and field-surveying, were also in some degree pleasing to me. But Euclid's Elements, arithmetic, and logarithms, were my aversion, as well as merchants' accounts. This latter I was so foolish as to consider illiberal and un-gentleman-like; fit indeed for a tradesman, but useless to one who was determined to be a soldier, that is to say, a hero, and of course a general!

My desire to be a soldier, or my desire of military glory, or my pride, was so steady and immoveable, that it swallowed up many other follies, and was, I believe, in the hands of a gracious Providence, an instrument of much benefit to me. From all my classical reading of amusement at school, viz. Rollin, Plutarch, Virgil, (and Homer, in English,) besides innumerable romances respecting love and glory, I gathered that glory was the great and only adequate object of every noble soul; that glory consisted in effecting the happiness of mankind, particularly of our own country; and that the means of accomplishing this glorious object were to be brave, temperate, just, disinterested, benevolent, generous, and wise. As I also felt a great desire and love for all these fine things, in speculation, I naturally concluded that I was in no small degree all that I loved and desired.

But I was beyond measure surprised and mortified to find, that these subjects, when proposed in this simple view to the generality of my companions, appeared to make little or no impression upon them; except in exciting ridicule at my folly and madness, as they termed it, in supposing that such things were true, or practicable; or, if practicable, any thing more than romantic absurdity!

The strong impression which was made upon my imagination, by the perusal of ancient history, poetry, and romance, soon displayed itself in the following manner. Among other books, I read Pope's Homer so often, and with so much pleasure, that I could nearly repeat whole books from memory; and at last I resolved to realize, if possible, those glorious scenes, which afforded me such rapture from the mere perusal. This purpose I at length effected in miniature, partly by example and kindling the fire of puerile emulation in the bosoms of my friends, and partly by the agreement of some wags, who sought for amusement in my folly.

That the minds of boys at school should frequently be vitiated by the perusal of books from circulating libraries, is not at all surprising, because it is very difficult to exclude them from schools in their vicinity; but I must own, that it appears at first sight wonderful, that an unreserved history of the Pagan Mythology, such as the School Pantheon for instance, which is in reality the Pandemonium of Milton, together with Ovid's Metamorphoses, should be given into the hands of boys*.

If the Holy Scriptures are the Word of God, then it is certain that the deities of the ancients were evil spirits. St. Paul declares, "*I say, that* "*the things which the Gentiles sacrifice, they* "*sacrifice to* DEVILS, *and* NOT TO GOD; *and* "*I would not that ye should have fellowship* "*with devils: ye cannot drink the cup of the* "*Lord and the cup of devils: ye cannot be par-* "*takers of the Lord's table, and the table of* "*devils.*" 1 Cor. x.

The Jews were severely punished for offering the bodies *only* of their children unto these idols. What then do we deserve, for offering the hearts and minds of our children to the same devils, as pourtrayed in Ovid and the Pantheon?

St. Paul says again, "*I speak as to wise* "*men, judge ye what I say.*" "*Behold Israel* "*after the flesh, are not they which eat of the* "*SACRIFICES,* PARTAKERS *of* THE ALTAR?" In

---

* The Reader will doubtless often perceive a degree of abruptness, and unconnectedness in the succession of many of my paragraphs. This defect proceeds in great measure from the chasms induced by the very numerous defalcations, and excisions of matter judged improper.

the same manner I would ask, shall not they who morally and intellectually *eat** the abominations of Ovid and the Pantheon, be partakers of, and digest the spirits of devils, of which these books are full, into their own souls?

Many readers will probably be offended by the display of the analogies used above; but I follow the example set in Holy Scripture, which explains spiritual things by means of their parallels in nature. In truth, it will be found at last, that there is no other mode of illustration, so quick, so clear, and so impressive.

The greatest misfortune which befel me at school, was the loss of all the sense of religion, imperfect as it was, which I gained at home. My guardian, indeed, was very strict and regular in the observance of religious rites, and obliged me to read the Bible, and attend the church, as well as family prayers, very regularly. But the benefit derivable from these two important points

* " Son of Man, open thy mouth, and eat that I give " thee. And when I looked, behold, an hand was sent " unto me; and lo, a roll of a book was therein; so I opened ' my mouth, and he caused me to eat that roll." Ezekiel, ii. and iii.—Again: " And I took the little book out of the " angel's hand, and eat it up; and it was in my mouth sweet " as honey: and as soon as I had eaten it, my belly was " bitter."—Rev. x.

of Christian discipline, was much counteracted
by the severity of my uncle. His mouth was
so continually the vehicle of abuse, and his
eyes of flaming anger, that when he preached
the divine doctrines of meekness, humility, and
charity, they came much distorted and disguised
through such a medium; so that I attended
more to the odious manner, than to the amiable
matter. Certainly, their good effect on me
must have been much weakened and counteracted, by his exciting at the same time the
opposite emotions of disgust and aversion towards himself.

But when I was at school, which was ten
months out of twelve, the impiety, lewdness,
and blasphemy, which were almost universal
there, soon produced the same things from my
heart, and quickly drove all religious thoughts
from my mind.

Upon the whole, I was speculatively an
admirer of all the virtues except humility, or
consciousness of unworthiness. It was impossible at that time for one who thought very
highly indeed of his own merits and dignity, to
be at the same time humble. No, I despised
humility with all my heart; for my proposed
models, the Greeks and Romans, had not, to
my knowledge, placed it among the Virtues, or
in the Pantheon.

Having thus given the best account of myself that I am able to do with a regard to my reader's patience, I shall dwell no longer on my school-days; but only observe, that the romantic sentiments of my heart, watered as it were by my irrational and polluted imagination, produced amphibious opinions and actions, incongruous and ill matched images of virtue and vice, ancient and modern, which puzzled all those around me, and did also long time confound all the investigations of my not half-enlightened reason and understanding.

Most assuredly also, I should have continued to wander for ever by the insufficient light of this opaque satellite, *human reason* in accumulated error. I should not have ceased (as Milton represents the Adversary, in his voyage through Chaos) to fall down for ever and ever, into the never-ending depths of the infinite abyss (for such are the depths of the divine wisdom and judgments, to the point of human reason), had not *the light of the Sun of Righteousness and Revelation* arisen on me with healing in his wings when I least expected it. Blessed for ever be His Holy Name. Amen.

PART THE SECOND.

" Is Israel a servant?   Is he a home-born slave?   Why
" is he spoiled?   The young lions roared upon him,
" and yelled, and they made his land waste; his cities
" are burned without inhabitant!"
" Hast thou not procured this unto thyself, in that thou
" hast forsaken the Lord thy God, when he led thee
" by the way?   Thy own wickedness shall correct
" thee, and thy backslidings shall reprove thee; know
" therefore and see that it is an evil thing, and bitter,
" that thou hast forsaken the Lord thy God, and
" that my fear is not in thee, saith the Lord of Hosts."
Jeremiah, ii.

I was taken from school at about the age of
sixteen by my guardian, who intended, if possible, to get me appointed a writer to Bengal.
He had received the promise of this appointment for one of his sons, who preferred to remain in England ; and he hoped that this promise would be devolved on me; but in this hope
he was disappointed.

To effect his kind purpose, he used to solicit
his friends continually; and on these occasions
he generally took me with him, sorely against
my inclination. My whole spirit panted for

glory, my head and heart were full of the heroes and sages of Greece and imperial Rome. I longed only to gather laurels in the field of Mars, and despised my notion of a writer, whose object I concluded must be filthy lucre. For this reason I was highly pleased at his bad success; and what filled him with mortification, was to me a subject of joy and triumph.

These fruitless attendances were however often intermitted, during a period of near three years which elapsed between my leaving school and going out as a cadet to India. This important interval of time was murdered by me in field sports, in visitings, and all kinds of idleness; but chiefly in the delicious idleness of castle-building in the air.

Yet in the midst of all this folly and vanity, I received a visit from a glorious and unexpected guest; for living in a very regular family, strict in religious profession, and being constantly obliged to attend public worship at church, and family devotions at home, the grace of God expanded my heart by degrees to receive delight in religious sentiments.

But my youthful glow of religion was then, I believe, all from the heart and imagination. My head or judgment had little or no share in it. It was an ignorant, unreflecting, but grateful faith. Nevertheless, it had the good effect, for the time, to purify my heart and conduct, though it was full of unsuspected leaven of self-righteousness.

All my good and evil moods and fits, however, were soon swallowed up in the master passion of love; and of a very refined and exalted kind of love, when considered in a mere natural and moral light.

As my conduct in the course of my idolatry (for all my affections were idolatrous at that time) was quite correspondent to the general romanticity of my character, I apprehend it will be best to say very little on the subject. Being now persuaded (in 1794) that it happened, and was overruled by a good Providence for my good, so it was of such a singular nature, on my part, as not to induce any permanent connexion; but only to purify my heart for a little season, previous to my launching into the world and its various dangers; and to make me feel by the most lively contrast, which also left me without excuse, how superior were the attractions of a pure, innocent, and genuine love (however romantic and platonic), to those vile attachments which I was afterwards to form.

My affection for this young lady had the character of the most tender friendship; heightened, no doubt, by the difference of sex, but completely that of knight errantry, or Quixotic romance. During the three years that I adored her, I do not believe that I once ventured upon the profanation of pressing her hand; neither did I ever descend to any thing so gross and indelicate (as I esteemed it) as to make a declaration of love. But my most animated attentions, my readiness to do or suffer any thing for her sake, were so obvious, and so obsequiously, so idolatrously devoted, that it was impossible for her not to see and understand them. In short, I then considered an amiable virgin, as an image of divinity, and her favourable and enchanting smiles as my heaven.

Beyond this, which I actually possessed, I thought of nothing! I desired nothing! Marriage, in any other view than that of perpetuating the bliss I did then enjoy, I cared not about. My soul doated upon her soul, as I saw it through the medium of her body! But in the course of time, I found that all her family, herself not excepted, supposed that matrimony was my object. This was a mistake; but yet, when it was brought under my consideration, I found that it was necessary that I should examine the subject.

The more I reflected the more I was confounded. How could a young fellow just come from school, and expecting to go out a cadet to India, think of marrying? Besides, her mother had forbid me the house. We had no fortune, either she or I. A stolen marriage would be madness; and what was to become of my military ambition? Could I thus begin my career at the point where it ought to end? How could I maintain a wife, who had no maintenance for myself? How could we offend all our friends? In short, the more I debated the matter, the more impossible it appeared to be.

I was relieved from these very troublesome and overwhelming thoughts by the absence of my idol, who, with her whole family, went to visit some relations in a distant county. In the mean time my sister returned from abroad, with her husband, a post captain in the royal navy; and the joy of meeting and residing some time with her, whom I had not seen for many years, tended greatly to banish the image of my idol. This passion, however, was much weakened by my discovering that she had no respect for romance, or platonic love; and it received a fatal shock during my residence in London. There I formed new acquaintances, who introduced me to the theatres, and, before long, to some of their female friends in Drury Lane and Covent Garden.

These dangerous connexions defiled my mind immediately, and, like a filthy garment, soiled and spotted the clean linen, in which religious affections had for a little while clothed and purified my spirit.

But I return to my sister and her husband.

They both declared that I was a young fellow of too much spirit to be made a writer of, and that I ought to be nothing but a soldier or a sailor. They advised me to say boldly to my old guardian, that I would be a soldier, and nothing else. Much persuasion was not necessary to induce me to do what was so accordant to my own wishes; and therefore when I returned to my guardian's house, and he called upon me as formerly, to attend him in his circuits of solicitation on my behalf, I told him very plainly, coolly, and firmly, that I was determined to be a soldier, and therefore that all this trouble was useless, and that I must decline going any more.

At first he appeared to be as thunderstruck at this unexpected opposition, the first I believe that he had ever openly experienced from me; he then tried to overawe me; but in vain, for his day was passed. He was then unable to flog or cane me as formerly; and he had exhibited the foibles of his character to me in such strong lights, that I considered him as nothing more than the most weak, inconsistent, and ridiculous creature in the world. Perceiving, therefore, that he could not shake my resolution, he gave up the point, observing, that I was certainly destined to be food for powder; and that if a person was resolved to be a fool, there was no preventing it. But he was from the above-mentioned 'circumstance, and many others, so convinced him that his plans for me were impracticable, that he went directly to town, and got me nominated a cadet for India that very day; and also brought me home Muller's Works, and some other military authors, among whom Marshal Saxe and the King of Prussia were of course my favourites.

When on his return he informed me what he had done, and gave me the precious volumes, which to me appeared to be inestimable treasures, I then almost for the first time beheld him with much pleasure. Great and sincere thanks I gave him upon this occasion, and received his exhortations to study the books, with complacency, and a desire to comply with them; a circumstance altogether novel and singular between us.

The above seems to show clearly, how important it is to consider the particular turn and inclination of boys, in the line of study which we propose to them, with a view to a profession. Gold, iron, lead, silver, &c. must not all be worked and purified precisely in the same way*.

* I beg my Reader's pardon for being so often figurative, but it is a habit contracted from the study of the Holy Scriptures. Thus St. Paul says, 1 Cor. iii. "Ye are God's "husbandry, ye are God's building." Again, "other "foundation can no man lay, than that is laid, which is "Jesus Christ. Now, if any man build upon this _founda-_

c

But..with respect to higher objects, that is to say, morality and (or in) religion, it is still more important.

Hence it appears to me, that schoolmasters should be men of genius, knowledge, experience, philosophy, and true Christianity. They should know when to use *fire*, and when *water*, and how to separate the ore from foreign combinations, by skilful process of moral chemistry, in metallurgy.

Perhaps it may seem extraordinary to those who are prejudiced against certain words, as a bull is against a red cloak, that a person professing religion should recommend philosophy. But I do not mean that abstract philosophy of words, that " *vain jangling*," condemned by, St. Paul. I mean the philosophy of God's works, or the divine œconomy of nature. This, when it is subordinate and coadjutant to divine revelation, and always points to it, (as it always does when truly considered and interpreted) for instance, in the Parables of our Lord, his Apostles and Prophets, and even by many uninspired writers, is then a wonderful illustrator of, spiritual truths, and a witness for God, who owns it as his own peculiar mode of instruction,

" *tion, gold, silver, precious stones, wood, hay, stubble ;*
" every man's work shall be made manifest, for *the day* shall
" declare it, because it shall be revealed by *fire.*"

from the 1st of Genesis to the end of the Revelations.

Perhaps a similitude may explain my meaning more clearly to my musical readers, than
any other mode of expression. I therefore consider the illustrations of divine truths afforded
by the parables of nature and natural science,
as explained by analogy, in the same point of
view as the accompaniments of a piece of music.
The Gospel itself, is the grand subject and air
of the divine concerto of the universe; and I
would therefore compare it to the violino primo
principale, or the piano forte part of a sym-
phony. Now, although this contains the air,
subject, and meaning of the composer, and the
accompaniments by themselves are comparatively an unmeaning jargon, yet the part of the
violino primo principale, if played without the
accompaniments, would be less full and em-
phatic, and it would not be so impressive, nor
so well understood, by any means. In short,
the effect would be much less grand and captivating. For the harmonies resulting from
various synchronizing systems, viz. violins,
tenors, bases, horns, clarionetts, &c. &c. &c.
all coinciding in corroboration and confirmation of the musical truths and beauties of the
sublime subject, must, and do, give it a power
proportionate to the degree of their judicious
support.

When I turned over my books, I felt a great desire to fathom the depths of the mysteries of Algebra and Fluxions in Muller and Robins; but not having laid a proper foundation for it at school, I found it too hopeless a task. Then I regretted my former idleness. Yet I looked at them as an ambitious prince does at the distant province which he conquers in speculation, after he shall have subdued the intermediate districts.

In fact, the carnal student, or philosopher, and the literal warrior, are much more similar than the world in general seem to apprehend; for the philosopher is an intellectual warrior, and conqueror. The vain glory which they both seek is but seldom acquired, and, if acquired, is too often ruinous to their own proper dominions. Thus ambitious princes impoverish their own subjects, and depopulate their own provinces, in subduing their neighbours. In the same manner, vain-glorious philosophers cannot, generally speaking, conquer regions of knowledge and science, without oppressing and diminishing the poor but vital and useful people of their own souls; that is to say, the sentiments of humility, meekness, and charity, which are the true riches of the moral and intellectual kingdom *. Too frequently also they lose their

---

* Thus when our Lord in the Gospel invites the rich young ruler to part with his wealth in favour of *the poor*,

faith, in proportion to their acquisition of the *empty knowledge* of the *shadows* of *this world.* In this case, they are ruined by their victories! They gain, say, the world; and lose the best part of their own souls.

There occurred not, so far as I recollect, any thing of particular moment, or importance to the object of this narrative, previous to my embarkation for India, except a transaction which shows that all my supposed love of heroism and romantic virtue was a mere shadow, with no better foundation than a cloud; in short, a mere castle built in the air, and void of all practical use and benefit. I have recorded this testimony of my weakness and depravity repeatedly, to show the vanity and emptiness of mere human virtue; and I have as often erased it, from the fear of being considered as a monster of inhumanity, and from the false shame of discovering to the world that I had poor relations. I have said to myself, this anecdote will only prove that *your* moral virtue was nothing but vain

and to follow *his example,* I doubt not that he meant more than literal riches; I believe he meant the riches of the moral kingdom, as well as those of the natural kingdom; for the young man had been vain-gloriously displaying the former, viz. " *All these things have I kept from my youth up.*" He was therefore to part with the riches of his self-righteousness and self-dependence, in favour of poverty of spirit.

speculation; but it will not convince other sceptics that their virtue is no better than your's. Experience alone can do that for them, if it is indeed true.

I now add, that history, both ancient and modern, proves, that moral virtue has existed before and without the preaching of the Gospel; and has even stood very severe trials, without losing its weight in the furnace of affliction: but I would also observe, that *Moses* and *Elias,* the *Law* and the *Prophets, reason* and *con-science,* did and do prophesy until (or unto) John, or repentance *; and after *that* faith in Christ, or the kingdom of God, is preached. This in itself shows that unregenerate virtue, though mixed with moral faith, is not perfect, since it only leads to repentance †. All these things are good in their day and place, and all are the precious gifts of God. Only we must be cautious, not to prefer the less to the greater, nor the means to the end.

Upon the whole, I will venture to say, that a near relation of mine was in great distress, as I heard, in poor lodgings, and in an ungenteel part of London, as I understood. I was exhorted to go and find him out, and relieve him.

---

* In the original, Luke, xvi. it is Ὁνόμος καὶ οἱ προφῆται ως Ἰωάνυ· or " the Law and the Prophets until John."

† That is to say, John the Baptist, " *A MAN sent from God.*"

But I had no means of affording effectual relief, without making application to my old
cross guardian in the country. The particular
part of Holborn was not pointed out; and I
dreaded being seen in any dirty lane or alley, en-
quiring for a poor man of my own name, by any
of my genteel or dashing friends. Therefore,
after much debate in my own mind, pride, and
vanity, indolence, and false shame, prevailed
over the desire which I *really felt* to assist the old
man (whom I had only seen once in my life,
when I was a child. But I confess that he then
gave me half-a-crown to buy gingerbread; which
circumstance has pained me more than any
other recollection. It was like a worm in my
bowels, or a barbed arrow in my breast). I
therefore permitted the notice I had received
to pass away unheeded, and stifled my sense of
guilt, by the excuse of inability.

It is evident from the above, that my house
was built upon the sand. At the same time
I allow, that the mere profession of Christianity
might not have enabled me to do my external
duty; I only contend, that the spirit of it, which
is charity, or divine love, certainly would have
compelled me to perform both the external and
the internal.

I completed my own education by the study
of Pope's Essay on Man, for which I imbibed
a zealous and enthusiastic admiration. This

celebrated system of moral philosophy, and
also as it appeared to me of true religion, could
not be suspected as dangerous to truth and
happiness, because I found it in the libraries of
religious, as well as of polished, and every way
respectable men. But exclusive of this autho‑
rity, it was so conformable in many parts to the
philosophy of my school friends, the Stoics,
and to my own blind heathenish pride, that I
considered it as an infallible oracle, which I re‑
solved to consult upon all occasions, and square
my conduct by. Already it appeared to me
more rational and madly than the Bible. The
two following lines from this Essay convinced
me that this great poet and (supposed) philoso‑
pher was a staunch Deist :

> " Slave to *no sect*, who takes no *private road*,
> " But looks through *nature* up to *nature's God.*"

This appeared to me to be the perfection of
right reason and sound philosophy; and there‑
fore I concluded, that the few closing lines, in
which he slightly mentions faith, were nothing
more than an unwilling tribute paid, from neces‑
sity, to the prejudices and superstitions of the
vulgar.

During the voyage to India my religious
sense, if I had any left, was soon extinguished
by the conversation and manners of a ship. In
the first place, there was no chaplain, and con‑

sequently no public worship; and I was too
genteel and philosophical to perform it in pri-
vate: neither did I any longer think it a duty
to pray night and morning as formerly; for I
conceived that as the Deity knew much better
than myself, what was necessary for me; so to
pray to him for any thing, was a kind of presumption and impiety, as well as absurdity. I
began therefore in good earnest to live as if
there was no God in the world, or what was
very like it; for I concluded that he was much
too high to concern himself about such worms
as we are; that he had established the general
course and order of nature at the creation, and
then had left us altogether to ourselves, to act
agreeably to our reason and conscience, or to
suffer the natural and necessary consequences
of a deviation from them. I also drew the following inference from the above premises; that
there was nothing that man could do, which
could affect God; and therefore, that the whole
duty of man was included in the obligations of
morality. This duty, however, I resolved strictly
to fulfil in every respect during life; and I flattered myself that I should find this an easy
task, for I did not yet feel any inclination to
violate any of the social laws; on the contrary,
I felt myself inclined to love every one around
me (in speculation), and therefore concluded
that almost every other person had the same
mind.

The voyage of life, therefore, which lay before me in distant deceitful perspective, and overspread with the mists and clouds of my own erroneous opinions upon the objects before me, which my fancy formed into most lively beautiful phantoms of bliss, appeared to me in the light of a party of pleasure, in which I should only find so much pain, as was requisite to make my pleasure more perfect, by the opposition of variety, or momentary contrast.

I then laughed in the fancied superiority of my own wisdom, and enlightened understanding, at the dark and superstitious prejudices, as I esteemed them, of my old guardian, and all those poor praying canting fools, who had kept me so long in the chains of ignorance, and illiberal ungentleman-like bondage. I despised with all my soul all such base wretches as were deterred from evil by fear of punishment, or hope of reward, either temporal or eternal, and congratulated myself, with swelling pride, upon my love of virtue *for virtue's sake;* because I almost thought that virtue and myself were one. In short, Pope's philosophy, his Essay on Man, was become my creed, my bible; and I often repeated to myself the following lines with triumphant exultation :

" Who noble ends by noble means attains,
" Or, failing, smiles in exile, or in chains;

" Like great Aurelius let him reign, or bleed
" Like Socrates, that man is great indeed."

Such a man as this, I believed myself to be; and therefore, from the height of my imaginary superiority, I looked down with contempt upon kings. I then little suspected what I soon felt, " *he that exalteth himself shall be abased;*" but I certainly did, before long, experience a degree of abasement in my own mind and conscience, fully proportionate perhaps to the degree of my former vain self-exaltation.

When we arrived in India, on the 12th September, A. D. 1776, I was, as I have described, a disciple of Pope; and also desired, and had made some awkward attempts, to become a pupil of Chesterfield; not indeed with respect to dissimulation, which I despised, nor to seduction and adultery, which I considered as heinous breaches of the moral code; but only in the study and practice of the graces, which however I soon gave up after a few vain attempts, without understanding. Nevertheless, having, during a short period previous to my embarkation, frequented well-bred company in the middle ranks in England, I was prepared to meet the same manners in India. But I was astonished and disappointed above measure, to find the manners of Indian Society approach nearer to those of my school days, than to any thing else which I had ever experienced. I found, in short, that the manners of a gentleman were quite different things in England and in India; and that in the latter nothing could pass for such, which was not blasphemous, or lewd, or riotous, or predatory; that is to say, the public being the common object of plunder.

Truth obliges me to make this declaration, because these things had an effect on myself, which it is in my plan to notice; the same truth, however, requires me also to own, that those shocking manners are at present (1809) banished from among us.

For some time I flattered myself (in my simplicity) that perhaps some Scipio might be found, after whose instructions and example I might model my own conduct. I still remembered with pleasure what I had read at school, concerning the supper conversations of the ancients; of the Grecian and Roman generals, who amused and improved themselves and their officers, by the discussions of Military topics, by analyzing different orders of battle, and considering the conduct of other great commanders before them. I hoped to find something of this kind; but I soon discovered that I was looking for what had no actual existence *.

* I confess that I wanted to play the general, before I had learned the duty of the subaltern. But still this error was a weed which grew up with the useful fruit, of military ardour.

2

In this situation my love of military glory was useful. I saw plainly, that if I became a debauched, enervate, idle, sensual creature, like many others, I must give up all pretensions and hopes of distinguishing myself in my profession, which object required self-denial, and a contempt of luxury; and I therefore avoided, as far as lay in my power, all such company, as I would have avoided a house infected with the plague.

Providentially, I loved reading, had still some relish for drawing, and delighted in music; so that these occupations, together with the occasional study of the Persian language, were very useful for a time in preserving me from the destructive abuses which daily ruined the most promising young men before my eyes; either carrying them quickly to the grave, or else leaving them mere shadows of men both in body and spirit."

Yet I was not always able to keep clear of such society, which was then very general; so that by degrees I lost much of my dislike to the manners of this new world; and as our common center of gravity lay much nearer to them than to me, I became by degrees drawn into close contact with them. Nevertheless, providential headaches, and sickness, soon disgusted me, and convinced me that I must either give up my health or my company; I therefore acce retired again to my reading and music, and my cloud-built towers of military fame; which, however, became daily more obscure.

With respect to women, I fear I was not more virtuous than my neighbours; but I was often more prudent, reserved, and ashamed of my excesses. I often lamented the dreadful necessity (as I called it) which drove me to do what in my cooler moments I much condemned and despised, though not from religious motives. I often reflected with inexpressible regret upon my romantic love in England, which, wild as it had been, was honourable and beautiful, when compared with these degrading connections. I wished that it was in my power to marry, or to subdue my corrupt propensities altogether, which, if I could effect it, would be a noble effort and triumph of philosophy. But my increasing knowledge of the world soon drove away this notion; for I reflected, that I could not gain any honour and glory from such a victory, were I even able to effect it; but on the contrary should only expose myself to ridicule and reproach.

But I was for a time delivered from these entanglements, by the almost sleeping spirit of military glory. The Bombay detachment under the command of Colonel Leslie, consisting of one company of native artillery, six battalions of native infantry, one regiment of native ca-

valry, and five hundred Khandahar irregular
horse, was ordered in 1778 to march to the
Malabar Coast, crossing the Jumna at Calpee.
With much difficulty I obtained my removal
from the European corps to which I belonged,
into one of the native battalions which composed the detachment. Then I congratulated
myself! Then my heart swelled with confident
hopes of gaining such military experience, and
performing such exploits, as could not fail to
raise me to notice, and in due time to glory.

For a time my mind was so occupied with
military objects, as to leave little room for any
thing else; but as the bustle of my own inex-
perience subsided, and I began to look around
me, I found that my companions had leisure
for libertine pursuits, as well as for public
duty; and (I confess) my military zeal soon
sunk to the common level of those around me,
with respect to what is called *the sex*.

Yet I both saw and felt what was morally
true and decorous, and would have embraced
it, as I thought, had it been attainable; that is
to say, attainable without taking any trouble,
or making any sacrifice: but I had cast off the
whole armour of God, and full of pride, ignorance, and self-conceit, exposed myself naked
to the fiery darts of the world, the flesh, and
the devil. The latter I believed to be only a
bugbear, and the two former to be my friends;

and I therefore most justly became the dupe,
and almost the victim, of my extravagant folly,
blindness, and impiety.

My whole progress in libertinism was che-
quered with the vain efforts of philosophic
pride, dying away gradually, but still from time
to time making convulsive efforts to bear up
against the increasing inundation of corruption,
within and without, which assailed me on every
side, and at last (as I more clearly discovered
the depravity of all my neighbours, and the
vanity of my own principles) carried me rapidly
away in its then irresistible torrent.

Souls which are restrained from vice, merely
by pride and shame, resemble lakes, which are
contained and kept up to a certain height, by
banks of earth only. For pride and shame, that
is to say, the hope and fear of the world's ap-
plause and censure, can only act as a bank to
the natural corruption of the human soul,
through ignorance of the depravity of the world
around us; and therefore a little experience,
that is, a little communication through some
weak part, soon brings down the waters of the
lake of the mind to the common level. But Religion is a reservoir in a solid rock, which lasts
for ever, in spite of rats, and winds, and waters.

My hopes of military fame, in the mean
time, were not much enlivened by my experience and observation; for, upon the whole, I

found that the hopes of plunder, of promotion, of a lucrative appointment, or command, made up the sum total of the military ardour of nearly the whole of my acquaintances.

The course of the war threw the army, of which our detachment formed a part, either collectively, or in brigades, and corps, into situations which enabled me in some measure to judge of the military and heroic dispositions, if not of the talents, of many conspicuous characters; and I found that the issue did not always raise them in my estimation, nor in that of the army *. But it was not so much any incapacity or failure in any particular men that damped my hopes and raised my indignation; it was the gradual discovery, in proportion to my experience, that the seeds of heroic emulation, and public spirit, appeared almost wholly absent from every bosom; and that all men, old and young, great and small, pursued, worshipped, only filthy lucre, gross sensuality, and false glory; glory purchased by base connivance, vile participation, and servile flattery.

This discovery of faults in others did not, however, at all induce me to suspect that the

---

* There were some exceptions to the above remark; among which was Captain W——ch; who with a rissalla of our cavalry, and a battalion, very gallantly surprised and defeated the Mahratta Gunnaise Punt, with 4000 horse, and four pieces of cannon.

same, or worse qualities were to be found in myself; and therefore it only excited my indignation against society in general, and strengthened my retired habits proportionately. But an incident soon occurred, which gave the finishing stroke to my remaining good opinion of the world, and left me, in the midst of society, as desolate and solitary as a traveller benighted in the depths of an immense and unexplored wilderness.

To enter into a detail of this incident would occupy unprofitably too much of my reader's and of my own time. Suffice it to say, that I discovered one of my intimates to be, as I thought, an unprincipled rogue, in a low style, or what is called a blackguard. Full of pride, rashness, and self-conceit, I communicated this discovery to him, supposing that he would resent it as a gentleman is bound to do by the laws of false honour; and feeling gratified by the idea of fighting a duel, in so honourable a cause as I supposed it to be. But my friend knew the world much better than I, and found it very inconvenient to expose himself to be shot by such a rash and foolish zealot in the midst of his thriving plans to make a fortune. He therefore took no notice whatever of my communication.

This politic forbearance only raised my zeal and anger to a higher degree. These passions were also excited by a third person, a friend of both him and me, who was, if possible, still

more incensed against him, and not only communicated many dishonourable anecdotes of
his conduct, but advised me to report his beha-
viour at head quarters, promising to assist in
the prosecution; which he also did. I therefore reported his conduct to the commander-in-
chief with all the solemnity and vehemence of
heroic indignation; he was in consequence put
under arrest, and tried by a general court martial. In those days, general courts martial in
India, or at least in our army under General G.,
were very different things from what they are at
present. Prosecutors were not permitted to be
in court after they had given in their charge;
neither were they permitted to submit any
charge, which was not approved by the court.
Fortunately for the prisoner, one of the charges
was peculation, or an attempt to defraud the
Pay Office. When I began to open this charge,
I was immediately silenced by the court; and
on my making a second attempt, I was ordered
out of court, and not again permitted to enter.
What passed therefore I know not; but the result was the entire, and, I think, honourable
acquittal of the prisoner.

He was pitied by many who were not ac-
quainted with circumstances, for having become
connected with such a dangerous enthusiast;
but those who knew us both thought me only
imprudent and romantic, but declared their

conviction that my motives were pure and honourable. 1 thought so too at that time; but
I now see that my purity was only a fancy, and
my honour was ignorant heathenish pride.

After this event I was received with such
shyness and reserve by many of my former acquaintances, as showed me too plainly that
they disapproved my conduct, and my notions
of honour. In consequence of this experience,
I retired more than ever from our world, which
I began to regard even with horror; and as I
had left England before I had found opportunity
to make similar observations and discoveries
there, I concluded that the circle into which
my fate had cast me was the most profligate in
the world. All my former bright visions of
glory were then completely obscured, all my
hopes seemed to be extinguished, and even my
wishes were for a time absorbed in resentment,
disdain, and despair.

Permit me, gentle reader, to venture a reflection or two, in this place. It now, in 1822,
appears to me wonderful and mournfully ridiculous, that after all the various discoveries
and detections which I had made at different
times, of my own weakness and baseness, I
should be able so entirely to forget all these hu-
miliating piercing convictions of condemning
truths, as to become thus vain, proud, self-con-
ceited, and blind; even really to imagine myself

to be heroically virtuous, and a noble spirit; and upon the strength of this self-delusion to set myself up for a reformer and public champion.

Yet if I had been left to myself, I should probably have contented myself with telling the young man my opinion of him, and then dropping his acquaintance. But I was stirred up by one older and more knowing than myself, who had imbibed a fixed contempt and aversion for his character, and we sharpened each other.

Upon the whole, it is evident, that " *the* " *heart is deceitful above all things, and despe-* " *rately wicked : who can know it ?*"—Jeremiah.

The violence of the various emotions which rent my heart was inexpressible, on finding that all my plans of glory and felicity, built on the foundation of the opinions of the Greeks and Romans, some thousands of years before, and as seen by me through the medium of romantic fancy, were entirely incompatible with the actual course and practice, as well as the opinions, of the present world. Yet there was no room for doubt or hesitation in my own mind concerning the truth. Generosity, public spirit, integrity, honour, and glory, must, I thought, be realities, Godlike realities! In truth, they were my IDOLS of *gold* and *silver*, which I devoutly worshipped in general like other heathens, and only rebelled against them on particular occasions of a sifting

nature. But the idol of the modern world, in
which I moved, was wealth or avarice, was,
in short, all the objects of selfish reason procured by wealth. These were stronger than my
childish gods, and were victorious. At that
time, however, though I felt its force, yet I
understood nothing of the mystery or theory
of this truth. It was a riddle too spiritual*
for my carnal mind then to solve.

I was, indeed, persuaded, that my speculative love of all the heroic virtues was just, was
even a divine afflatus. I also still flattered myself, that I possessed inherently, and self-suffi-
ciently, the said *splendid* qualities of moral *gold*,
silver, &c. because I perceived certain brilliant
points, stars of light, in my imagination, which
were really at an immense distance from me,
but which I most childishly conceived to be
close at hand, and even in the center of my
heart. Hence, I, as it were, thought myself
to be in heaven, or heaven *(the divine qualities)*
to be in me, though I was in reality upon the
brink of hell, and ready to fall into the depths of
the bottomless pit, of my own deceitful unbeliev-

---

* By spiritual the writer means, abstracted from material
objects, or intellectual, or metaphysical; and lastly, in a
religious sense, either legal or evangelical. For the law is
spiritual, as St. Paul says; and I consider myself authorised
to use the word as freely as he does.

ing heart; and this was my farewell view of
the regions of light. These regions, however,
were only those lower polluted heavens, which
Paul calls " *the beggarly elements of this world*,"
(Galatians) and in which reigns " *the prince of*
" *the power of the air*," Ephesians; that is to
say, the human, moral, vain-glorious virtues.

With respect to the indulgence of my sensual
appetites, I indeed thought it unphilosophic, un-
heroic; but as this was clearly not the age of
heroism, and as I found myself too weak to stem
the torrent of society, I resolved to indulge
them, that I might not run mad for want of an
object to occupy my roving restless mind; but
which I resolved should not be the base object of
the world's idolatry; money, or self in its lowest
form. As I admitted not the existence of any
divine law, or revelation, or any possible offence
against the Deity, independent of moral obligations, and as I thought I had an undoubted
right to dispose of myself as I pleased, within
the pale of my own morality; so I met with no
obstacle to this last resource, this ultimate (or
rather and happily penultimate) enquiry after
happiness, in the search of which, I had been
so long disappointed. Here my reader may
say, I thought you had been experimenting in
this way for some time. I answer, only eventually and incidentally, as an auxiliary, not as a
principal.

Thus having long worshipped the host of
heaven, that is to say, those distant brilliant
points of imaginary goodness and virtue, which
I met with in ancient history; and which I
fixed in my own mind as the limits of absolute
perfection, or *heaven;* finding also at last that
they were beyond my reach in the actual state
of the world, I was forced to descend reluc-
tantly from this superb idolatry, and to devote
myself to the worship of things in *the earth be-*
neath; that is, the corrupt and inflaming images
of *creeping things* (lusts) in my own *heart.*
This I soon did with a vengeance *(a divine ven-*
geance); not suspecting that as earth joined to
heaven on one side, so it was connected with
hell on the other. Here, again, my reader may
say, laughing, I thought heaven was on every
side, all around; pray, on which side is hell?
I answer, on the side of the *center;* the center
of the *wicked heart* is *individual* hell.

Amongst various whims which entered my
mind, long puzzled and confounded in the vain
search for truth, among the tombs of error;
where I was continually wounding myself with
stones which I supposed precious (that is to
say, pride and hardness of heart), which I considered as virtues, it occurred to me to reperuse
the Scriptures called sacred; and I expected
much amusement from the shrewd remarks
and ingenious discoveries which I conceived I

should certainly make in analyzing this wonderful book, this mountain of superstition, as I
esteemed it. With this profane view I took up
the Word of God; not at all doubting the full
sufficiency of my own understanding to comprehend it, if it was consonant to reason, or of
my ability to judge accurately whether it was
true or false; because I conceived that reason
was the sole judge in this case, as in every thing
else, and that whatever was incomprehensible
to reason must be false. Thus, I took for my
foundation this capital error, that I was possessed of right reason ; whereas I was wholly
destitute of it; for my understanding was blinded
by thick prejudices, and bound in the chains of
pride and infidelity. Neither did I in the least
doubt the goodness and purity of my own heart,
whose fine moral sense I depended upon as a
sure guide in all cases of conscience. Thus the
maniac in his dark cell, seated on stubble, and
bound with iron and brass, supposes himself to
be a king seated on his regal throne *.

. Deluded as I was by impious pride, and
hardened in unbelief, the sequel may be readily
foreseen. After reading a very small portion of
the sacred volume, it appeared to me so contrary to reason, justice, humanity, and even to

---

* I forgot, or despised, the admonition of Solomon, " *He*
" *that trusteth in his own heart is a fool.*"—Proverbs.

common sense, in many respects, that I did not
hesitate to pronounce it a gross imposture, a
palpable and impious forgery. I was chiefly
astonished how it could possibly have been so
long imposed on the credulity of mankind as a
divine revelation. Being therefore more convinced than ever, that all revealed religions
were human fabrications, invented by priest-
craft and kingcraft, to lead mankind by the
nose, and make the multitude of simpletons a
prey to a few artful and selfish individuals, I
was filled with indignation against the whole,
but (alas) more particularly against Christianity,
because I dared to think it the most impious and
tyrannous of any*!!!

Moreover, I did not believe that the penalties of revealed religion were necessary to bind
mankind, and preserve the order and peace of
society. On the contrary, I was persuaded that

---

* I must now add, that the writer of this Narrative, after
the above-mentioned examination, and insane and impious
judgment, concerning the Holy Scriptures, and the Christian faith; consummated his blasphemous madness, by seizing the sacred volume in a rage, throwing it upon the floor,
and out of the house!!! And yet this shocking reprobate
still lives, and believes the same glorious volume to be the
very word of God, and desires, hopes, and prays to live and die
in this blessed faith and obedience, as the only truth, and
name, and way, given to mankind, whereby we must be
saved. Amen. Glory be to God, the Father, the Son, and
the Holy Ghost. Amen.

pure deism was the only thing that could possibly revive the delightful scenes of the golden age, and render the whole human race a band of brothers, united by the ties of rational freedom. For what was so beautiful, so true, and so clear, as virtue and benevolence, if fairly represented, if divested of the disguise of *black superstition?* The necessity, therefore, of Revelation, or superstition, which were to me synonymous terms, seemed to my mind a positive falsehood, a popular error, sanctified by time, and founded on ignorance, by selfishness; but which, thanks to the aid of *reason*, the only *true prophet*, the only *real revelation* from heaven, was now vanishing apace, and would, as I trusted, be wholly abolished in a very short time. This blessed and glorious period I anticipated in my imagination, with all the ardour of a Voltaire, many of whose pieces I had devoured.

I thus became persuaded, that the depravity of mankind proceeded chiefly from the abuses of religion; which at the best, or in those who did believe it, I regarded as a little good mixed with a great mass of evil, and a clumsy substitute for the beauty and purity of virtue. I conceived that the evil was then come to its greatest height, but that the vulgar were too gross and ignorant to perceive the true cause, which it was reserved for such philosophers as the above men-

tioned and *myself* to discover, and also to display, as I hoped, for the good of mankind.

Here I paused, and, from the summit of this
mountain of pride, looked down with pity,
mixed with self-complacency, on the world below.
I resembled the star-gazer, who fell into a pit,
while busily employed in settling the affairs of
the heavens, and wholly inattentive to his own
paths.

As I made no other use of the gifts of God
(that is to say, my speculative love of virtue
and benevolence, which doubtless were intended
to lead me to the truth of Christ) than to turn
them into idols, and then into devils, which I
worshipped; and made him no other return
than to apostatize, and blaspheme his name and
word, and join myself to his enemies; so, he
at last (I suppose) gave me up to my own heart's
lusts, and to the temporary dominion of those
evil spirits, whom I chose for my gods, and
exalted above his word in my heart and mind.

I must here forbear to relate a singularly vile,
insane, impious and scandalous frolic, which I
committed in a Portugueze Church, full of
images of saints, which had been converted into
a magazine for military stores, during the siege
of Basseen, near Bombay. But why should I say
one? I must omit many, in which were combined almost every degree and kind of blasphemy, sacrilege, indecency, and reprobracy!

I had indeed soon ample cause to repent most bitterly (had my eyes been opened) of these most grievous insults, which I had so publicly offered to every law, whether of religion, morality, or decency. From that time forward, I became more rapidly and desperately vicious, gross, sensual, and almost devilish; for though my bodily powers were exhausted by abuse, yet my imagination was still active, and ran through all the chambers of imagery——!!!

At length my dreams became so unspeakably dreadful, that I sprang out of bed, and from downright terror attempted (for the first time during several years, I believe) to pray for protection: but yet the blindness and hardness of my heart were so great, that, like Pharaoh, I still refused to believe (in spite of all the plagues with which the divine justice and mercy permitted me to be infested) that the old wives tales, as I had been accustomed to think and call them, respecting hell and the devil were true. At the same time I was burning in the fires of hell, and possessed and tormented by a legion of evil spirits.

In vain I called my former speculative love of glory, honour, and romantic virtue, to my aid. These vain idols were gone; they were weak as water, they were distant as the stars, they were as chaff carried away by the wind. Yet I sometimes thought more justly; and then it was clear

to me, in spite of Satan's philosophy, that virtue
and vice were not mere modes and fashions,
invented by men, to suit different climates, and
various prejudices; but that they were eternally
opposite principles, placed by a divine hand,
together with happiness and misery in their
train, within our view, and according to the
choice of our hearts within our reach. Yet this
being the case, as I felt it was from experience,
I admired for what end it was ordained, that we
poor miserable worms (for I no longer esteemed
myself a hero or demigod) should be formed
thus capable of becoming vicious, and, consequently, miserable! Why not make us absolutely and unalterably good? How could I help
my corruptions? Did I at all foresee them when
I began my career of sensual pleasure, closed,
alas! in torments?

Such were my vain and erroneous reasonings,
and such was the living death in which I dragged
on a miserable hateful existence, when the Lord
of mercy beheld me with undeserved compassion, and raised up a judge and preparatory
deliverer for me, who, though unable immediately to break my chain, did yet make it so
intolerable, so like red hot iron, that my soul
was completely roused to combat and resist, to
the utmost of her power, the increasing horrors
of spiritual death which were gathering fast
around her. This stern judge, and in some de-

gree deliverer, by making me strive to be delivered, was the *scorpion conscience*, whose burning sting gave double force to my torments.

From such misery as I experienced, I could find no remedy, but death in some form; and as, in spite of my supposed philosophy, I was still too much of a coward in infidelity, to venture to commit an action, which seemed so final and irretrievable as suicide, I therefore resolved from that day to contend with double diligence and perseverance against my corruptions, and rather to die a thousand times in any other way, or by inches through my incessant and cruel torments, than ever again admit, or entertain for a moment, imaginations which I found, by terrible experience, to be so dangerous, so subtle, so penetrating, and so difficult to be effaced from the memory.

In consequence of this incessant and fiery warfare within me, my existence was become a dream of horror, a dreadful burden, a curse as it were full of bitterness and wrath. When alone I was absorbed in anguish the most intolerable. Every sentiment of my heart was converted into a scorpion, all which, by turns, pierced me with pangs that cannot be described.

How infinitely merciful were all these chastisements! Had they not been inflicted, and in such an exquisite manner and degree, I should certainly have been lost for ever. But

my conscience being (unknown to me) supported
by the power of God, gave me no rest. It was
an incessant thorn in my paths, and made them
so grievous, that I was absolutely forced, in
spite of my thoughtless and idle habits, to study
how to assuage its torment; and my false pride
and shame, though supported by Satan, were
too weak to overcome this mighty witness for
God, and were therefore obliged finally to
submit.

Experience convinced me by slow degrees,
that my only remedy was to resist the wicked
licentiousness of my imagination with all my
might in the first instance. This, for a long
time, I found to be an Herculean labour; yet by
dint of perseverance, and a determined resolution to die rather than be conquered, I at length
(by the grace of God through Jesus Christ our
Lord) found that I had made a little progress;
and to assist this as much as possible, I came to
a resolution never to be idle; for I found that
the tempter (by which I mean my evil thoughts,
for as yet I perceived nothing beyond them)
always took advantage of me in such moods,
and prompted me to all kinds of evil.

The next alleviation to my misery I found
to be humility, and submission to the rod of
heaven, which I began to be in some measure
sensible of. I was indeed at last forced, in spite
of myself, and my secret enemy, to feel, and

see, that God was not, as I formerly and blasphemously thought, an almost indifferent spec-
tator of wickedness, but that he clearly saw it,
and as surely punished! This great and important truth was burnt as it were into my heart,
by the actual cautery of conscience, in such an
intolerable manner, that my soul, subdued by
exquisite torment, was forced to bow herself to
the *dust* of acknowledged *error*, and the *dunghill* of *vileness*, and humbly and tremblingly
supplicate a remission from her agonies.

In this manner I for some time kept up a
weak fight and resistance to my spiritual foes,
without knowing who they were, or who it was
that supported me; seeking by all means to
keep my mind constantly employed in reading,
writing, music, and every employment which
might help to drive away the evil spirit that tormented me; and I found so sensible a benefit
from these occupations that I followed them still
more and more.

I was about this time (1782) called to a
situation, which gave my enemy an opportunity
of tempting me on another side which I had
always considered to be my forte. My strong side,
as I vainly thought it, was my love of justice,
my public spirit, and contempt of filthy lucre.
I was appointed paymaster to a large corps of
troops, and entered upon my new office with
hopes of emolument which I did not formerly

feel. But though, through the undeserved pro-, tection of God, I escaped from any open actual breach of probity and honesty, yet my desire of making a fortune, (which desire had hitherto been dormant, from the interposition of those dreams of glory which possessed my heart, and were to be blown away in the first place, and secondly from the absence of temptation and opportunity) this desire now increased with the nearness of the attracting object, which appearing to be within my probable reach, attracted my heart in a proportionate degree. At the same time, I suppose I may do myself the justice to say, that when I accepted the office of paymaster, I resigned a still more lucrative appointment attached to it, which was that of commissary of stores to the troops : this I did because I understood that I could not reap the full emoluments from it, without overstepping the boundaries of what I considered to be the duty of an honest servant of the public. The two under-commissaries in this department did not see the matter in the same light; and they, therefore, very readily took all the trouble for the sake of the emolument.

At the close of my paymastership, by which. I really made nothing, but what I saved from my open allowances; I was called down to Calcutta on the business of the office, to assist in settling the accounts with my predecessor and senior, for whom I had partly been acting. Being also by a train of incidents introduced into the gayest society there, the incessant cry of the watch-dogs of conscience was the only thing that could have possibly preserved me from ruin, amidst the great dangers and temptations to which I was continually exposed : had my conscience slept in this time of general assault from every quarter, I should have been lost.

But here, again, God's providence raised up this judge and deliverer, this Samson * for me, who was so much stronger than the giants of the Philistines, that he overthrew them even in their own cities. By this figure I mean to say, that the power of reason and conscience was so great within me, that it put to flight my pride, vanity, and uncleanness of thought, even in the midst of the most intoxicating pleasures, and the gayest company. Neither the charms of beauty, the delicacies of the table, the inspirations of wine, nor even music itself, had any power to support me against the overwhelming force of this inexorable judge within; whose just decisions often pierced my heart with the acutest agonies, almost to fainting, when I

---

* Is not the history of Samson, like that of Abraham and his family, an allegory ? I do not mean allegory *only*, but allegory *also*, as well as literal and historical fact.

tried to appear most full of mirth and joy. In vain did I pour down bumper after bumper, to drive away, if it were possible, my misery, by intoxication; my conscience defied the power of wine; and I only filled my veins with fuel to feed the fire of that tormentor, without being able to overcome its terrible voice.

My particular situation at that time riveted these chains, these cart-ropes of fashion and vanity upon me, too strongly to be broken through, until the business was finished which brought me to Calcutta; but then I was preparing to withdraw from a society of nominal pleasure, but vanity, snares, and real misery, when an unexpected incident brought me back, for a time, to the same tiresome and dangerous round. The second grade in a high military office was conferred upon me through the friendship of an officer, who had formed an opinion of, and regard for me, much higher than I merited; and as we were old acquaintances, I lived with him at his desire. This situation threw me back again into all the dangers from which I had been about to escape.

But far gone as I was in the paths of error and perdition, my deliverance was approaching, and even near at hand. The accidental absence on business of the officer in whose quarters I lived, left me more at liberty to spend as I chose those hours which were not devoted to

official business; and I often took advantage of
this circumstance to amuse myself much more.
rationally and profitably at home, with the
study of the Elements of Euclid, than I could
have done in vain and dissipated company.

My ambition, my love of military glory, had
indeed been much cooled and damped by experience, and diverted by other pursuits of sensual pleasure and emolument, which I found to
be full of snares and thorns; but it now revived
in great force, and became, in the hands of a
merciful Providence, the instrument by means
of which I was gradually rescued from perdition. I found that theory, as well as practice,
was necessary to form a good soldier, which I still
ardently desired to be; and I saw plainly that
the shortest way to acquire a theoretical knowledge, was to sit down seriously and regularly,
and go through a course of mathematical
studies. It also struck me, that such a course
would more effectually than any thing else
divert my attention from those dismal visions,
which had so long rendered my existence a
dreadful burden; and from which I could find no
deliverance in what the world called pleasure.
Animated, therefore, in the highest degree with
the delightful prospect of effecting two such
important objects at once, and attracted also
very strongly by the growing taste which I felt
for such speculations, I made immediately a

firm resolution (which I was enabled to keep)
that I would devote myself to this one object,
from that day; and that I would wholly reject
every consideration or temptation whatsoever,
that should at all interfere with this determination.

Finding then that I could not prosecute this
plan, without resigning my appointment in Calcutta, I instantly resolved to give it up; and I
accordingly did so, as soon as my friend returned, in spite of the advice and remon-
strances of all my well-wishers, who were by no
means proper judges of an action whose motives
they could not penetrate. They were naturally
surprised at my resigning a post of eight hundred pounds per annum, besides free quarters
and table.

Having then resigned my office, I rejoined
my corps; and my new plan, being an untried
road to happiness, was trod by me with all the
ardour and enthusiasm of my natural disposition. Thanks be to God; for this was in some
measure the beginning of my return from spiritual captivity and bondage.

The difficulties which I encountered, at
setting out without a guide, only acted as a spur
to my diligence; I therefore persisted with un-
abating perseverance to study nearly all the
day; and when I quitted Euclid and my algebra,
it was only to attack the Persian language,

whioh I also included in my military plan, or
to take up my violin as a relaxation from
intense mental application.

As I thus proceeded, working out every thing
by my own labour, and comparing one branch
of science with another, I could not but perceive the strong analogy between the whole;
and that they were in fact only as different
languages, which expressed the same truths in
different modes. This discovery (for such it
was to me) excited my curiosity to trace this
very striking analogy still further and further,
and even to advert to it constantly, in the study
of all subjects whatsoever, that came under my
consideration. Accordingly, the more I examined and compared, the more clearly I was
convinced, that mathematical truth, as in the
Elements of Euclid, was the common basis,
the real, though hitherto to me unsuspected,
law of truth, reason, and proportion in every
line, in whatever direction; both in respect to
the objects of animate and inanimate nature,
and also in respect to the human heart and mind.

By attending to arguments of any kind with
this clue in my head, I still perceived the same
things. All was to me like geometry. I saw
that the truth of every subject was a mathe-
matically straight line, surrounded on either
side by imperceptible curvatures of error, of
different degrees of excentricity, which were

adopted as straight lines by disputants, according to the degree of the clearness of their understandings or mental sight at the time. I also perceived that this greater or less clearness of sight depended ultimately upon the *feelings* of their *hearts*, which either elucidated or obscured the operations of the understanding by the coolness or heat of the passions at the time; and that the same persons who reasoned truly, when unbiassed by inclination, argued in downright opposition to the plainest mathematical demonstrations, whenever their *hearts* became interested on the other side*. I also observed, that those who could clearly see these inconsistencies in others, were almost blind to the same things in themselves; and I therefore gave myself credit for being as blind as my neighbours with respect to my own failings.

Hence I laid it down as a moral theorem, that the heart was the source of all our errors; and therefore, that the difficulty of discovering the truth with respect to our own selves, was almost if not quite insurmountable by any human being; because it depended on his being able to abstract himself from himself; on his being able to remove, as it were from his own

---

* Because feeling is demonstration to the heart; and when that demonstration is strong, it rejects with indignation the demonstrations of the intellect.

center of gravity, beyond the sphere of the attractions of his own heart! so that in physics a man might as well attempt to rise above the moon in our solar system.

In short, the more I studied human nature through the medium of analogy, the more entirely I was persuaded of its weakness, blindness, and depravity. I saw plainly, that but few men, comparatively, either approved or disapproved from love of the truth, but merely from the corrupt bias of the heart; which, by its strong attractions of lust and selfishness, obscured and misguided the rational understanding; as Omphale is said to have fascinated the son of Jove, making him to spin with her maidens: or as " *the Danite strong*" was besotted by Delilah, and by her betrayed to the five lords of the Philistines, who blinded him! Even thus is the understanding mind cajoled by the sorceries of the passions, and delivered up to the dominion of the carnal senses, which are five tyrannic lords, by whom reason itself is blinded.

About this time, I learnt by letters from my sister in England, whose husband had died, that she was in great embarassment, owing to the unexpected failure of some of her annuities. This intelligence cut me to the quick; for, not even suspecting her situation, which she had concealed from me as long as possible, I had

squandered away all the profits of my two
posts, as well as my military pay and allowances, upon dancing-girls, and kept mistresses:
in maintaining a crowd of idle, useless, dishonest, and profligate servants; in giving extravagant entertainments, and musical parties:
so that when I reflected upon the sums that
were spent, and the foolish manner in which
they had been consumed, I was quite overwhelmed for a time with vexation at my own
folly, and a sense of guilt, for having thus
abused the valuable gifts of Providence.

Being at length roused to serious reflection,
and to take some effectual steps towards the
relief of my sister, the first retrenchment which
I determined to make from my current ex-
penses, was the stated sum which I had hitherto
allowed my mistresses. I accordingly parted
with the one whom I at that time maintained,
and resolved, if it were possible, to abstain
from all such connexions from that day forward; not because I esteemed them irreligious,
but only unsatisfactory and inconvenient. This
appeared to me by no means improbable, because I felt then a great degree of indifference,
to say the least, to every thing of the kind; and
most providentially I was enabled to persevere
in this resolution so far, that I have not thus
offended since that time (viz. 1788).

A celebrated poet says, justly,

" Habits are soon acquir'd ; but if we strive
" To leave them off, 'tis being flayed alive."

So I found it by experience. For a considerable time after I ceased to keep, my corrupt
propensities appeared to have gained double
force from being restrained. Yet the unknown
grace of God enabled me to persevere. It
was, however, impossible for me not to be sensible, at particular times, that the loud impor-
tunity of my carnal corruptions proceeded
partly from the want of discipline in my diet.
I therefore made it a standing rule, which I
never would break through, not to eat supper.
I found the great advantage of this regulation
very quickly, both in body and spirit, which
became more cool, well tempered, and peaceful.
The former was less rebellious; and the latter
was more clear, serene, and rational.

After I had persevered some time in this
course of comparative temperance and chastity,
I perceived, with high satisfaction, that I had
made a sensible progress. Being therefore persuaded that my speculation was perfectly practicable, and that perhaps I had already sur-
mounted the greatest difficulties, I was fully
encouraged to persevere, and reap all the valuable fruits of my abstinence, small even as it
was. These, as I have mentioned above, were

2

not only corporeal, but also mental. They
consisted partly in a clearness of understanding, and a kind of spiritual discernment*, which
made me every day, I knew not how, discern
more and more the beauty, harmony, divine
wisdom and goodness, displayed in all the visible
works of God, and their relation and analogy, or
proportion, with the invisible things of my own
soul within me. I found, in short, that there
was not any natural object upon which I could
reflect with rumination, (if I may be permitted
to use the expression) without finding a wonderful resemblance in it to some quality, or faculty,
or operation of the heart and mind; and that all
the works of creation spoke the language of
reason, and moral truth, in different modes
suitable to our different organs, through which
they were conveyed; but that they were ultimately the same things, almost infinitely varied
and repeated.

In this manner, the whole creation, so far
as it was brought within my sphere of mental
vision, was gradually converted into an im-

* By *spiritual*, I do not mean *evangelical*; I mean the
united action, or co-operation of reason, imagination, and
sentiment, under the guidance (as I believe) of the spirit of
truth moving on the chaos of sin and infidelity. St. Paul
speaks of a spiritual *mind* as well as *heart*; also of spiritual
wickedness, as well as of spiritual *holiness*. In short, he
uses the word in its proper metaphysical sense, and not in a
partial view.

mense table covered with food and medicine
for my soul. Thus was I gradually and un-
consciously, every day, approaching nearer and
nearer to the light of divine truth, and to true
happiness.

I continued to prosecute my studies, and
comparison of *spiritual* (or, perhaps I should
say, of moral and intellectual) things with
natural things; and as I gained intellectual
strength and clearness by degrees, I extended
my researches by the help of natural science
and philosophy, beginning with the most beautiful and attractive subjects. My fondness for
poetical beauties, which I considered as a kind
of natural inspiration, *under the divine appointment,* made me take greater pleasure than ever
in reading Thomson's Seasons; a book that I
had always greatly admired, but in which I now
perceived and tasted a thousand newly-dis-
covered beauties.

Among other works, I was delighted exceedingly with a fragment of *Le Cat's* Essays on
the Five Senses, or, as I esteemed and called
them, the five *languages, doors,* and *avenues* of
the soul, the *gates* of the *human metropolis;*
where reigns *the head,* or *king,* of the whole human system. I apprehend that David means
ultimately the same thing when he speaks pro-
phetically of " *the gates* of the daughter of
" Zion," who in a mystical sense is the *king's*

wife. Of all the senses, I think it may be said
that they are " *alter et idem ;*" that is to say,
as much as one language is like to another in its
meaning and ultimate scope, although they are
different in form. They show our hearts, as
well as our minds, *what* is within us, by inducing
comparison of it with those shadows or images
of the same things, which we thus continually
and variously, or in manifold forms, receive from
without. Thus Solomon, who was the greatest
master of the mysteries of analogy that ever
lived, and by an acknowledged divine gift, says,
" *Also, he hath set the world in their heart, so*
" *that no man can find out the work that God*
" *doeth from the beginning to the end.*"—Ecclesiastes, iii. For none but God can know the
whole heart, or the whole earth, or world, from
center, to the extreme circumference of the creation; or, as the Scripture says, "*from the be-*
" *ginning to the end.*"

   In short, it pleased God, who seeth not as
man seeth, and who worketh all things after
the pleasure of his own will, and who leadeth
the blind by a way which they knew not, to
open gradually the eyes of my understanding,
and to let me perceive a little part of the universal analogy subsisting between all those
different modes or languages; I also continued
to believe that they were all founded in mathematical proportion, which I therefore concluded

to be a universal basis and law for all the different operations of matter and spirit, because I thought it was absolute truth, or the law of God.

Hence I became more firmly persuaded continually, that all visible and invisible things had their parallels, or at the least their near resemblances, in the opposite scale; perhaps perfect, but at all events much more so than was in general supposed; for the above mathematical law of truth and proportion, or in other words of rational intellect, pointed out that things which were similarly measured by one and the same thing must of necessity be very similar *inter se*.

This persuasion so stimulated my desires to discover the first general principles of truth in all things, whether visible or invisible, that I resolved to pursue my mathematical researches much further than I had at first thought of, and to qualify myself for a familiarity with all the grand discoveries of Newton and other philosophers.

Such was my situation, and such were my views, in the pursuit of which I expected to enjoy the truest happiness that this world could afford; for they appeared to be highly rational in themselves, and also highly conducive to the purity of my heart, the illumination of my mind, and the peace of my whole soul. I was

by this time fully convinced, both from reason
and sentiment, from theory and the most ample
experience, that there could be no true felicity
independent of virtue; and I conceived that my
studies tended highly to strengthen all the virtues, by discovering not only their positive
beauty and excellence, but also the meanness
and vileness of their opposite vices.

With respect to the defilements and horrors
of my evil conscience, which still at times tormented me like a never-dying worm; finding
that I could only prevail to mitigate them, but
that they were absolutely unconquerable; that
they were not to be expelled by any human
power*, so I regarded them as a just and divine
punishment for my manifold wickedness; and
expecting no less than to suffer them during life,
I endeavoured to submit with humility and patience to the justice of the all-seeing judge;
hoping that the torments which I was thus destined to endure in this world, would be deemed
sufficient to expiate my offences, and that the

* I felt this by my own experience; but I was unable of
myself to discover the only true remedy, the true Balm of
Gilead, as it is figuratively called; that is to say, the blood of
Christ sprinkled by faith upon the guilty conscience.
Neither did my infidel ignorance and blindness then permit
me to know that all the torments I could suffer, and all
the efforts which I could make in my own strength, in the
course of ten thousand years, would be unavailing to wash
away even one of my sins. For every sin is a mortal wound.
Cure one, and you may cure all!

continual efforts which I was resolved to make to purify my heart and mind, would, from the great mercy of God, be accepted by him, and introduce me to happiness pure and eternal after death.

Such being my fixed, and as I thought un-, alterable plan, I determined, in consequence, to quit as much as possible a vain, blind, and deluded world, and to devote the remainder of my life to those scientific, and equally to me moral pursuits, which alone appeared to promise me any solid rational hopes of happiness. But the very wonderful mercy and infinite goodness of God my Saviour, whom I had hitherto denied and blasphemed, had prepared a better portion for me, even in this life; which I shall describe, as far as I am able, in a separate part, or division.

PART THE THIRD.

" I waited patiently for the LORD, and HE inclined
" unto me and heard my cry. He brought me up
" also out of an horrible pit, out of the miry clay,
" and set my feet upon a rock, and established my
" goings. And He hath put a new song in my mouth,
" even praise unto our God: many shall see it, and
" fear, and shall trust in the Lord.—Psalm xl.

My reader has seen how, by the infinite and
undeserved grace and mercy of God, I was
drawn up from the depths of the pit of my own
heart's pollutions, snatched like an half-con-
sumed brand out of the fire of hell, and enabled
to retrace, step by step, the path of destruction. He has also seen, that in proportion as I
ascended to revisit the air and light of heaven,
my deeply-rooted corruptions and foul stains
were purged off by proportionate rays of celes-
tial light and heat, and by the balmy zephyrs of
divine grace, which were operating, unknown
to myself, in my heart and mind. I indeed
thought, that the blessed, though gradual
change which was going on in me, was the
mere natural and necessary result of my own
efforts; but still I was thankful to heaven for

that knowledge and experience, which had roused and forced me to make them ; and I fully resolved that they never should cease during my life.

In consequence of this resolution I was diligently employed, according to the plan which I have related in the foregoing part, when my peaceful studies were interrupted, and all my schemes of knowledge and retirement overturned, by the breaking out of the late war with Tippoo Sultan, A. D. 1790.

This important event roused more completely the spirit of military ambition, which, as before observed, was only dormant, but not extinct, under the load of sensuality and vanity, which had been gradually reduced to ashes in the furnace of affliction. This ambition was of a more modest and humble degree than it had formerly been ; for I did not now swell with the vain hope and desire of becoming a hero, a model of military perfection, but only proposed to perform a duty. Yet I resolved, before I would either indulge or repress the rising ardour of my heart, to consider the matter coolly in the balance of reason and conscience.

In the first place, I was persuaded that as a soldier, it was my duty to neglect no opportunity of acquiring such professional experience, as might eventually render me useful to my country ; and I therefore considered it to be

my duty to endeavour to be present in this war,
so very likely to afford me ample experience and
instruction, although I was not immediately called to it by the voice of external authority. I felt
indeed very considerable regret at the idea of
quitting those studies which afforded me so
much pleasure and information; but I was
conscious that mere speculation without practice was of little use, and that if peace was the
time for study, war was equally the season for
exercise. I therefore considered, that the period
was arrived, to reap the fruits of my mental application, and perfect my newly-acquired
theory by actual experience. There only remained therefore one point to be examined;
which was, the justice of the war in which we
were engaged.

Had I been called in tour of duty to bear
my part in this expedition, there would have
been no room for hesitation; obedience being
the first duty of a soldier, where it does not
evidently and clearly militate against his undoubted duty to God: but as my action was to
be voluntary, it also behoved me to see that it
was just. When I had, therefore, satisfied myself by inquiry and reflection that our cause
was a good one, I resolved to embark in it; and
I in consequence made application to Lord
Cornwallis, through the military secretary Colonel Ross, by my friends, to that end. After

making strenuous efforts, I had the mortification
to be refused to go even as a volunteer; and had
given up all hopes of success, when: a vacancy
happening in one of the corps, I was appointed
to fill it, and thus got removed to the detachment which marched to the Carnatic under
Lieutenant-Colonel Cockerell.

Upon receiving this intelligence, I left all
my effects in the hands of a friend, to be sold
by auction; and being already prepared for
such an event, I set off with all possible expedition from Benares, to overtake the detachment which had already marched from Tamlook
and was near to Midnapoor. I went down in
a small boat to Calcutta, tracing the route
of the detachment, in a manner conformable
to the ardour of my desires, having neither tent
nor horse but a palqui, which served me only
as a bed, and house; for the bearers, taking
advantage of my situation, would not entertain
with me, except under the express stipulation,
that I was not to ride in the palqui, except in
case of dangerous sickness. To this hard bar-
gain I was forced to submit; and, as the detachment had got so great a start of me, was obliged
to make very long and fatiguing marches of
often thirty miles a day, sometimes without any
halts, in order to overtake it in convenient time.

The good providence of God, in which I
indistinctly trusted, though not through Jesus

Christ, was graciously pleased to carry me safe
through all dangers and difficulties; and I over-
took the detachment, near to the temple of
Jaggrenaut, without any other disagreeable experience than that of burning heat, and exces-
sive fatigue, which had reduced me almost to a
skeleton.

I had taken care to bring with me a treatise
of algebra, and my Euclid's Elements, which I
used sometimes to call *my bible*, meaning by
that expression, *a system of pure and undoubted
truth;* but without clearly knowing that it was
a true type of the law of spiritual truth, as far
as Moses can take us without the Gospel; and
in the study of these, and some other mathematical and military books, I passed my solitary hours, which were rendered still more
heavy by my sore reflections on my own depravity, and that of society in general.

But the active scenes which soon took place,
served to divert my anxious thoughts, and to
relieve those painful feelings, which otherwise
would have pressed too hard upon me, considering that I had relinquished that course in which
I expected to receive the truest satisfaction.
Yet I found so much spare time, that I was
enabled to go through quadratic equations, and
enter upon cubics in my algebra. I also gained
a peculiar, *and so far as I know* an *unique* sight
of the nature and spirit, or meaning of alge-

braic operations, which was very useful to me afterwards, in a degree which I did not altogether anticipate at the time.

In reflecting on what passed all around me, with a view to my spiritual, or moral and intellectual researches, I still perceived as formerly the partiality and iniquity of human nature, its predominant selfishness, and its quicksightedness to the faults of others. I saw that the natural consequence of all this, was a continual increase of selfishness and misanthropy; in short, of all the misery, error, and wickedness, with which mankind were overwhelmed. Finally, I saw that the great, deep, and horrible foundation of the whole system of evil, was *the infidelity of the HEART, and of the HEAD, with respect to God and goodness;* the *aberrations* of the latter, proceeding chiefly from the *aversion* of the former. My own life was to me a wonderful proof of this proposition, most clearly and practically demonstrated; and every thing that I experienced, was a fresh confirmation of the same truths.

I was then persuaded, that I had at last solved the riddle which had formerly puzzled me so much; and as I was convinced that if I could but explain and demonstrate it, and its consequences to the world, as clearly as I saw and felt it myself, I should, perhaps, be the means of happiness to thousands, I was inspired

with an ardent and vehement desire to sit down
seriously and regularly, to this great and, as I
supposed, most beneficial undertaking.

. I had an imperfect yet strong conception,
that all moral and religious subjects might be
discussed, illustrated, and even demonstrated
in the same way, and with as much clearness,
as mathematical truths; and that the laws of
geometry, or natural truth, bore a very close
resemblance to the laws of reason and moral
truth. For both the natural and moral worlds
were the work of one author; and both were,
or must be, measured by one and the same rule
of right reason and proportion. Truth must be
the one law of both, though in a manner conformable to their different natures; but its
operations in both must have the same character,
the same tendency to constitute and build up.
I had also an embrio conception, that the
wonderful science of algebra had a peculiar,
and even a more distinct, and if possible, more
striking reference to the same things; and that
it would, upon more particular consideration and
comparison, afford me an excellent assistance
in my arduous undertaking. Concluding, therefore, that if I could establish true religion * and .

* By this time, I had advanced so far, that I supposed
true religion to consist in the belief of one God, supreme
and omnipotent, who loved virtue and benevolence, and

morality upon the basis of mathematical demonstration, I should, as it were, annihilate at once the source of all vice, and therefore of all moral evil and misery, I was consequently enraptured with the captivating prospect of my own imagination *, and resolved to execute my project on the first opportunity; and in the mean time, most diligently to prosecute my mathematical studies, and the views which arose continually from them relative to, and illustrative of, the correspondent truths of morality and religion.

Stimulated in the highest degree by these motives, I was completely avaricious with respect to time; and even when I was detached on picquets and outposts, always had my algebra or some such book with me, that I might not lose a moment. Yet such was the constant

hated vice and selfishness; and who would certainly reward the one, and punish the other, at least after death: who was continually present to superintend the course of the world, and all mens' thoughts as well as deeds.

* My Christian reader will smile here, at the darkness and shortness of my spiritual or religious views; for I was so ignorant, at that time, of the human heart in general, and of my own heart in particular, as to suppose that the knowledge of the truth would be fully sufficient to ensure the practice of it, by all persons of common honesty. Perhaps, this may appear almost incredible to some; but it is nevertheless true, and only proves how completely I was deceived by my own heart! " *The heart is deceitful above all things,* " *and desperately wicked: who can know it?*—Jeremiah, xvii.

occupation of my attention and time by the course of the campaign, that I had no leisure to enter upon the pleasing task which I meditated, until after the return of the army from our first, and unsuccessful, attempt against Seringapatam.

I had by this time been removed into a battalion of volunteers commanded by an old friend, which battalion was thrown into winter quarters in the Fort of Oussore, lately taken from Tippoo Sultan. It was during the time of my residing in this place, that, finding a considerable degree of leisure on my hands, I began to enter upon the execution of the great plan which I had so long projected in my imagination. My first efforts were very feeble ; and I plainly felt all the disadvantages that I laboured under from the want of a solid foundation of erudition, which I had so much neglected at school, and the value of which I was now enabled to estimate, by the importance of the subjects that I wished to demonstrate and recommend, and my deep felt inability to do them justice.

Nevertheless, it was necessary to make a beginning; I therefore, at last, came to a determination to set off with an examination of all the duties of morality: first, their absolute necessity even to the consistence of human society, and still more to its purity and felicity; and secondly, of their entire connexion

with, and dependence upon, religion; that is to
say, their divine origin, revealed in and to man,
by the voice of reason and conscience ; thirdly,
their resemblance to, and agreement with, the
nature of the Deity, as was manifest from the
testimony of those His witnesses in us, and
from his otherwise glorious display of his divine
attributes, in the works of nature, and the
laws of natural science. All these appeared to
me to speak the language of religion and morality, in different modes and forms, but in one
and the same spirit of truth ; clear, rational,
sentimental, and mathematical truth !

From hence, I deduced the following obvious
conclusion : that as all the works of God, both
animate and inanimate, expressed the very same
things, though in a thousand different tongues,
some positively, and some negatively; and as
they all with one voice pointed from EARTH to
HEAVEN, in a regular and connected scale of
gradual ascent, from grossest matter to spiritual essence: that therefore this testimony of
universal nature, was in a figure, and in truth,
the voice of God, and to be considered as a
revelation truly divine. That as this revelation,
this innumerable host of witnesses for God, all
declared that He loved truth, and all the moral
virtues; and that He equally hated all the opposite vices ; so it was clear to demonstration, that,
being omnipotent, He would certainly reward

what He loved, and punish what He hated as enemies to truth and goodness, and happiness. I also naturally inferred from the frequent pros- perity of vice, and the oppression of virtue, in this world, that God being the principle, the fountain of truth and goodness, was, as it were, bound by the law of his own nature, which was immutably perfect, to bring all things to a proper level in the world, to come; and, therefore, that a future judgment was equally demon- strated with the being and attributes of the Almighty.

Such were the outlines of my first plan, which wholly excluded all particular systems of re- ligion, all partial revelations, as fables and human fabrications; and which I proposed to bring to the perfection of mathematical demon- stration, through the sole paths of pure deism. Full then of my subject, down I sat and wrote my thoughts and sentiments upon the moral duties of man, feeling clearly in my own mind, as I went on, their necessary descent from, and relation to, GOD; and their *reasonableness* as well as *self-evident beauty ;* the first being DE- MONSTRABLE, the latter SENTIMENTAL, or by feeling.

Hence, I clearly distinguished the different modes of operation of these two great witnesses for GOD; viz. REASON and SENTIMENT, LIGHT and HEAT, the HEAD and the

HEART; the *first* proceeding by the way of speculative demonstration, through the gradual medium of the *understanding*; the *second*, and more rapid (as being more independent of man), appearing to be an inmate and inherent capability in *the heart*, (bestowed by the fountain of goodness and beauty) to distinguish in an instant, yet passively, or by perception of feeling, apparent good from apparent evil, beauty from deformity, symmetry from disproportion, both natural and moral; the first being *shadow*, the latter being *substance*. Because, from the original * perfect construction of all things in truth, it was necessary that all *evil* should excite *antipathy*; that is, appear deformed, and feel painful to a good and pure sentiment; and all *good*, by the same law, was necessarily sympathy; that is, appeared beautiful and proportionate, and felt pleasing to the same good and pure sentiment.

I then endeavoured to show by various examples and cases, which I thought in point, particularly with respect to the *human form*, that the natural cases of beauty, or deformity,

---

†. By original is not meant here, the original creation of all things; but the original, unsophisticated, undebauched, genuine sentiments of the heart of every individual, before he is corrupted and vitiated by communication with a selfish and meretricious world: I did not then believe any other fall of man.

were only shadows or figures of the moral *;
and that they were intended chiefly as directors
and indices, to lead us on by degrees from the
investigation of natural truth and beauty, to
those originals, those realities of the moral and
spiritual world, which were the true light and
life of heaven, only typified by the others. " I
strove to prove, that mathematics in general
were similitudes of the law of reason in man;
and that all works of taste and beauty, were
only as shadows of the moral beauty perceived
by imagination and sentiment; and that to
suppose, that the capability of investigating
the glorious works of the Creator was given to
man chiefly for the use of his body, which was
almost brutal, in preference to the information
and improvement of his soul, which was related to the Deity, was a positive absurdity, a
perverted and inverted ratiocination, which
tended directly to degrade man altogether into

* Not that I was so uncharitable, or so very ignorant of men
and things, as to suppose, that a beautiful form would ensure
a lovely spirit; or, that a deformed person was a necessary
accompaniment of a vicious distorted soul! No, I only saw
that in the natural scale, natural beauty and symmetry were
truly emblematic of, and proportionate to, that state in the
soul, or the spiritual system, which we consider to be lovely
and rational. But parallel lines are not coincident, or one and
the same; but only, beauty : natural things : : grace : spiritual things, and symmetry : natural things : : reason and truth
: spiritual things.

the image of a beast. I contended, that it was
greatly by means of this absurd abuse of reason
and sentiment, that mankind were become so
depraved. I supposed, that the ingenious re-
finements of scientific luxury were the high-
water mark of this depravity, which, if not
checked by effectual judgments, must in the
natural and moral course of events (as I concluded) induce the destruction of the whole
world.

I then lamented the errors and blindness of
modern education, which (as I thought) almost
wholly overlooked the regulation of the heart,
on the proper cultivation of which every thing
(under God) depended; and aimed only at
cramming the mind with learning, useless, and
even pernicious, without duly regulated affections. Warmed by my subject, I then launched
out in praise of the noble characters of antiquity; yet such was my blindness and wicked
prejudice, *that I placed Socrates first in my
list*, and after him *the Saviour of the world*!
I concluded with the praise of *Howard*, whom
I supposed that Providence had raised up in
these latter times, lest all the sages and heroes
of antiquity should, by the increasing depravity
of the world, be shortly considered as merely
fabulous and unreal characters.

Nevertheless, as I proceeded, my understanding and my heart were gradually so recti-

fied by the spirit of truth, that I became convinced of my error, in placing Socrates at the
head of my catalogue of inspired mortals;
(which I was persuaded that all wise and good
men were). I therefore erased his name, and
inserted that (now adored one) of JESUS
CHRIST, as the most perfect and worthy of
mere mankind. Thus I rose one step in my
creed; viz. from pure deism, to a kind of Soci-
nianism, or Unitarianism.

Thus far I had proceeded, when my speculations were interrupted by the call of military
duty. My corps was ordered out of garrison,
and employed from October to December 1791
in active service in the field, together with two
others, one of which was a king's regiment.
After taking by assault a fort of Tippoo's on
plain ground, we proceeded to attack the strong
and almost inaccessible hill-fort of Kishnghur
in the clouds. Here we were repulsed, after
losing the greater part of the light company,
and some of the grenadiers of the King's regiment, which led the column of attack according to the etiquette of military precedence.
For though the forlorn hope got up to the foot
of the wall with the ladders which they
planted; yet these were found not to reach
much more than half-way up to the top! So
deceiving is the appearance of the heights of
walls at such an immense elevation.

3

All the mischief was done by stones, or rather masses of rock, which being pushed over the top of the parapet, where they had been previously placed, swept away every thing on the road (which they commanded) over the brink of a tremendous precipice of some hundred feet, after crushing their bones to pieces in the first instance.

Here, it may be asked, why does the writer insert this solitary scrap of military narrative into a work professedly evangelical in its object.

I reply, not to please myself, but to gratify a particular friend, who begged hard for a history of my campaigns; but as this would be quite foreign to my views, and would, I apprehend, make a mixture something like oil and vinegar; I therefore only insert (as it were) this patch, to show how awkward such a composition would appear.

My corps returned from the service it had been employed on in December, and was destined to form part of the garrison of Bangalore; and so soon as we were settled in our quarters, I again resumed my former unfinished work.

Being convinced from a long train of reflections and observation, that the body of man was merely an image or shadow of his soul, I began to write an Essay on the subject, comparing the one with the other, member with

G

member*, in all cases that fell under my observation, or resulted from my own experience; and though I felt a considerable difficulty in setting out, and a great deficiency in point of physiological knowledge; yet as I proceeded, step by step, fresh lights were continually thrown on the subject, and confirmed by the living manners of society, in such a clear and striking way, as equally surprised and delighted me, and made me admire from whence such lively demonstrations, and yet of so abstruse and spiritual a nature, which I neither gained from books, nor oral instruction, could proceed. This has since that time frequently brought to my awakened mind (or some will think dreaming mind) that mysterious passage of promise and consolation to penitent sinners in Isaiah, viz. " *The children*" (of the† soul) " *which thou* " *shalt have, after thou hast lost the other, shall* " *say again in thine ears, The place is too strait* " *for me: give place to me, that I may dwell.*

* Thus, to instance very briefly, abstract *reason* is the head of the soul, and *sentiment* or moral *feeling* is the heart and blood. The *stomach* of the soul, which digests its food practically, is the *understanding* of experience, or resulting from experience. Therefore in Scripture *reading* and *understanding* are figuratively called *eating* and *digesting.*— See Ezekiel; and Revelation, x.

† The children of the soul, from the premises, are clearly the generations of its *thoughts* and *sentiments ;* of which, as in a little world, there is a continual succession, from the birth to the grave.

3

" *Then shalt thou say in thine heart, Who hath*
" *begotten me these, seeing I have lost my chil-*
" *dren, and am desolate, a captive, and removing*
" *to and fro? And who hath brought up these?*
" *Behold, I was left alone : these, where had*
" *they been?*"

Here I was again interrupted in my speculations, by being detached in the beginning of
January 1792, with two companies of sepoys
under my command, to garrison a small hill
fort, taken from Tippoo Sultan, called Ram
Ghurry, and one of the dependencies of Saven-
droog. This retired situation was enlivened by
the society of a very agreeable young officer,
who commanded one of the companies, and,
like me, was fond of poetry and literary amusement. The first month of our residence in
this post, was spent in putting it into a state of
defence; but when this pleasing labour was
over, I again employed all my leisure, in the
prosecution of my plan.

In the course of my reflections, which I
committed to paper, it became clear and manifest to me, that the human soul was in itself
both male and female; and when arrived at
maturity, was truly represented in bodily
shadows by the state of matrimony†. That as

* The experience of thirty years shows me, that this
intricate subject will not be properly understood by readers

man and wife were one flesh, so the head or
mind, and the heart, became united into one

of any description *(almost)* without some further elucida-
tion, and bringing more force of Scriptural evidence. In
adducing this, I must of necessity enter on the limits of
metaphysical inquiry ; and therefore, I would entreat the
patience and candid allowance of metaphysical adepts, in
the event of my using terms, which they may judge not to
be appropriate to the things which I mean to describe. For
instance, the words *qualities, faculties, powers, heart, mind,
soul, spirit, affections, passions, intellect,* &c. It is probable, that I may not always use the above terms with pro-
priety, agreeably to the newest edition of metaphysical definitions, by the great masters. All I can aspire to, or hope
for, is, merely to be understood ; and even that may be a
presumptuous hope, considering the abstruseness of the
subject, and the incompetency of the writer.

My intelligent and critical reader, if he takes the trouble
to consider the subject, may, perhaps, perceive a degree of
confusion and perplexity arise in the course of the developement of the analogies of the above similitude. This I also
felt and saw after a little consideration; but I did not so
soon find how to obviate the difficulty. Thus, *the human
head* is pronounced by St. Paul to be the type, or figure or
emblem, of *our Lord Jesus Christ;* and the rest of *the body*
to be emblematic of *the church, his mystic wife.* But this wife,
though she is female in a collective point of view, in comparison with *her husband the head,* is yet composed of *both
male and female* ingredients, or individuals, in pretty equal
proportion.

Now, if we suppose, (what seems to be a reasonable sup-
position) that the types, figures, and parables, set forth by the
inspired writers, and by our Lord Jesus Christ, are (generally speaking) perfectly accurate and congruous in all their
parts to what they represent, then we may lawfully infer,

spirit or soul; and that as the object of matrimony was the propagation of healthful chil-

that the human body, which is the Scripture emblem of the
church, is in all probability congruous therewith, in all respects of true proportion, or analogy. Hence, we may
reasonably look out for a parallel in the human body, and
soul, also, to the *male* and *female* component parts of the
church, as characteristic of the sexes.

If any person can point out any other more comprehensive, striking, and important characteristics, than reason
and the intellectual faculty altogether, including the imagination subordinately; and sentiment, or feeling, affection,
passion, and all moral perception; then I shall give these up
and adopt his characteristics; but as the above include both
the mind and heart of man, which are the vital organs and
functions of the soul, or, as it were, the whole essential of
man; so I must beg leave to keep to them, until some faculties more important, and more characteristic of the sexes,
shall be presented.

Now although *men* have *sentiment*, or *heart*, and *women*
have *rational intellect*, or *mind*; yet I apprehend that man
is (generally speaking) more intellectual than woman; and
that woman is (generally speaking) more sentimental than
man. If this be allowed, and if it be required to give a
brief characteristic of each sex, in mutual relation and
comparatively, then intellect seems more characteristic of the
man, and sentiment or feeling more characteristic of the
woman. But St. Paul himself says, 1st of Corinthians, xi.
chapter, " *Nevertheless, neither is the man without the woman,*
" *neither the woman without the man, in the Lord;*" or, in
spiritual truth.

Among a multitude of characteristics of man and
woman, given by the celebrated Lavater, chapter xxiv. on
male and female characteristics, he says, " *The female thinks*
' *not profoundly; profound thought is the power of the man.*

dren, to be educated in virtue to happiness;
so I supposed the final cause of making the

"*Women feel more; sensibility is the power of the woman.*"
This testimony from so competent a judge, together with
the common sense and observation of mankind, which, so
far as I have read, heard, and seen, do correspond with the
opinion of Lavater, make me venture to hope, that perhaps
I have succeeded in my endeavours to discover in the individual human soul, faculties, or properties, which are
parallels to the distinction of sexes in the church at large.

With respect to *the body* however, the fact has not yet
been established; for though the heart is common both to
soul and *body*, meaning in the first case the organ of the
affections, and in the latter the organ of the blood; yet the
bodily organ corresponding to the human mind or intellect,
has not been specified, much less demonstrated. Let us
then search for it.

In the first place, all will agree that two of the most
important and vital organs of *the body* must be selected, to
represent the united whole. The heart is already admitted
as one, and where shall we find another organ *in the body*,
so important, and so vital, as *the lungs?*—The lungs! ex-
claims my reader in surprise, I thought you had already
fixed upon *the head*, or *right reason*, as the *male*, and as *the
husband* of *the body!*

Very true, my gentle reader, the head, that is to say, the
emblem of Christ, is the husband of the whole body, as
one collective church. But you must also remember, that
this church is composed of male and female individuals, who
are also joined together, in individual matrimony among
themselves. This is the obscurity, the ambiguity, the
difficulty, the mystery, which long puzzled me. I confounded the two unions together, when I ought to have kept
them distinct; and I burdened myself with a distinct sub-
division, when I ought only to have considered the case in a

soul both male and female (or rational, intellectual, and sentimental) was its similar union

grand and comprehensive view, as St. Paul does in the fourth
chapter of Ephesians. He also says in chapter v. on the
subject of *individual matrimony* among believers, "*This is a*
"*GREAT MYSTERY, but I speak concerning Christ and the*
"*church.*" He also says, 1st of Corinthians chapter xi. "*The*
"*head of every man is Christ; and the head of the woman is*
"*the man.*" Therefore, every believing married couple is
one complete man, whose head is Christ; and lastly, every
believing individual man and woman contains, in a sub-
division of the subject, a miniature picture of the *grand*
whole; viz. the head of the *man,* abstract *reason;* the head
of the *woman, intellect,* with the *imagination;* and the woman,
or *lovely affection* and *just sentiment.* Only, in the woman
the *heart* predominates; and in the man, the *mind,* with
more of the great *head,* right reason, predominates. But
let us return to the consideration of the lungs.

As the natural heart dispenses blood, or natural life, to
the *sanguiferous system,* which is the undeniable type of the
mental system; so do the lungs in union with the heart dis-
pense air, which also is natural life to the same system. But
the *form* of *air* (or I should say, the mode of the agency of
air) is different from that of blood. Nevertheless, the
reality of the air is confessedly as real, and its necessity as
urgent, as that of blood.

But air is *invisible,* and blood is *visible;* and it is common,
though a mistake, to say, that *seeing is believing;* for St.
Paul says, "we walk by faith and not by sight." It is not
difficult to see intellectually, that the blood is emblematic
of the *affections;* for Solomon says of the heart, "out of it
"are the issues of life" (Proverbs); and *love,* or *benevolent*
affection alone, is *life* to *sinners.* But the analogy between
air and *intellect* is not so obvious to common observation.
Yet *air* is certainly emblematic of *spirit,* and *intellect* is

under the divine auspices ; that *rational intellect,*
the head, and just sentiment, and lovely affection,

spiritual. If not, then we are all material, and materialists.
But a man may say, that air is not emblematic of spirit, and
he may demand a proof that it is so.

Direct proof, in those very words, cannot perhaps be
given ; but circumstantial evidence may be collected in
abundance from Holy Scripture. The same word denotes
both air and spirit, both in the Old Testament and in the
New. This by a Christian should be, and will be, regarded
as strong testimony.

Our Lord " *breathed on his disciples, and said unto them,*
" *receive ye the Holy Ghost.*" John, xx. And the operations of the Holy Spirit are by our Lord compared to the
wind ; " *the wind bloweth where it listeth,*" &c.—" *so is every*
" *one that is born of the Spirit,*" John, iii. In the first
general Epistle of St. John, the three great witnesses for
God on earth, are said to be " *the spirit, the water, and the*
" *blood.*" The word used for spirit in the original is air, or
Πνῦμα. It is probable, that this ought to have been rendered
air, and not *spirit,* because *water* and *blood* are *material*
things, as well as *air.* Nevertheless, it does not much
signify to one who has been taught that all natural things are
types, because he will be enabled by faith, and by the grace
of the Spirit of truth, properly to arrange the various parallels he meets, without confusion.

In the first chapter of Genesis it is said, " *And the Lord*
" *God formed man of the dust of the ground, and breathed*
" *into his nostrils the breath of life ; and man became a*
" LIVING SOUL." Observe here, that the *breath* of life
is (or means) also the *spirit* of life ; for " *man became a*
" LIVING SOUL," as well as a *living body.*

The above evidence appears to be quite sufficient to
satisfy any one, who does not shut his eyes against the light

the heart, (or the spiritual male and female)
might under the influence of divine truth, or

of truth, in consequence of prejudices. Hence it will
perhaps be allowed, that as *the heart* is the organ of natural
blood, or life; and as the *lungs*, united with the heart, are
the organ of natural air, or life; also, that as the *blood* is
the emblem of *moral life*, or love, and as the *air* is the
emblem of *spiritual life*, or *truth in love;* so they are the
two grand members of *the body* which represent the whole;
in short, the types of *the male and female* component parts of
the individual soul, and also of the whole church at large,
under CHRIST THE GREAT HEAD.

But there still remains another weighty objection to
answer; not indeed weighty in its own merits, but in the
clouds of prejudice and unconsciousness which invest, and
magnify, as well as obscure it; and in the confidence, the
popular unchecked confidence, with which it is advanced.
It is asserted, or admitted by many pious persons, among
whom is the late excellent Rev. Joseph Milner, (in his
Sermon on the Brazen Serpent, as the Type of our Lord
Jesus Christ) "that types and emblems are *seldom* to be
"taken *strictly*." But he adds, " *very true,* neither ought
"they ever to be *explained away entirely*. They *seldom hold,*
"it is acknowledged, if we descend to *minute particulars;*
"but this instructive emblem would fail in its leading and
"most essential circumstance, if an eager longing sight of
"the Saviour on the cross did not perfectly heal the most
"inveterate spiritual malady."

But with all due deference and respect to the worthy
and eminent character above-mentioned (who, however, is
more *for* than *against* the use of types and figures), and all
other such, I would humbly submit, that every man's
opinion, who has an opinion of his own upon this subject,
will be formed by his own experience. Suppose a parable

the spirit of the Deity, propagate the offspring
of the soul, or vital truths, unto eternal life

of Holy Scripture to contain various distinct members or
branches, all capable of an edifying and apposite interpretation, though not all by any means equally obvious to every
disposition of mind.   Let any number of ecclesiastics endeavour to give the true interpretation of the parable.   It is
probable, that some one may only give the interpretation of
the most obvious member; another may interpret two, another three, and so on; until some one shall interpret the
whole truly.

Now, it is certain, from the nature of the human mind
and heart, that every one of these persons would form an
opinion to himself, concerning the interpretation of the
parable, different from every other in some particular; and
that this opinion would be determined by his own success.
When they came to compare notes, as it is called, those
who had made the most scanty interpretations, would call,
or think, the more copious explanations of their brethren
bold and fanciful; and intimate, with a shake of the head,
their apprehensions (quite unaffectedly) that they might
induce dangerous errors.

But are those who see least, to be always credited above
those who see most?   Yes; it will be answered, if the
former see through the medium of reason, and the latter
through that of imagination only.   But who is to judge of
this point?   The bird imagination soars to many heights,
which the reasoning elephant with all his force cannot reach.

My situation, in writing analogically, is somewhat
similar to that of the Hebrews making bricks, and building
cities in Egypt; and I perceive, that, as a writer on spiritual
subjects, I am in an evil case.   For I fear, from experience,
that my judges will consider my analogy as so much chaff, or
stubble, or at the best straw.   They require me to prove my

and happiness. I considered the actual present
union of my own reason and sentiments, as such

assertions without the help of this analogy; or, figuratively,
to make my figurative bricks, and to construct my figurative building, without using this straw, or stubble.

If I were to tell these judges, that analogy is " *a reed,*
" *like unto a rod,*" and that it is able to "*measure the temple*
" *of God, and the altar, and them that worship therein,*"
Revelations, xi. some would laugh, and some would frown,
and perhaps some would say, Show us how. I will therefore try to do so, praying for, and trusting in, the aid of
that Holy Spirit of truth which gave the parable, and who
alone can give a sure interpretation.

ANALOGY, or *proportion*, is an instrument, by help of
which we are enabled to measure unseen things, by means
of things that are seen. It is declared by my judges to be a
weak fragile instrument; yet they concede that it will measure worldly, temporal, carnal things, with general success;
but not spiritual things, or the connection between spirituals
and temporals. I contend, that it measures both.

A REED, is a weak fragile instrument; but if carefully
used it will serve to measure accessible magnitudes actually.
The external appearance is like that of a rod, as well as the
measuring use to which it may be applied; and it is so applied *mystically, to measure spiritual things by analogy*, both
in the Old and New Testaments, viz. Ezekiel, xl. and in
Revelations as above. *Consider this well.*

A ROD, in Scripture language, means *a measuring instrument, or a rule of true proportion*, which includes the
idea of chastisement for the breach. Thus *the law of Moses
is a spiritual rod*, and the natural rod that he bore was an
emblem or symbol of *the law*. Hence analogy, which measures both spirituals and temporals, and compares them
together (for instance, in the Parables of our Lord Jesus
Christ), however weak in itself, is like unto the rod, or law

a marriage; and these very truths, proceeding from the said union, to be the children so be-

of spiritual measurement; and by the help of faith is able to measure inaccessibles, by means of their proportion to accessibles, which it can actually measure.

THE TEMPLE OF GOD, in prophetical and figurative language, means both the soul and body of the Christian; see first of Corinthians, vi. and second of St. John's Gospel.

THE ALTAR of that temple is the heart, from which every sacrifice must be offered in order to be acceptable.

"THOSE WHO WORSHIP THEREIN" are they who worship in spirit, and in truth; therefore all these things are measured by the reed analogy, like unto a rod.

After all, a resolute objector may say, "this, at best, is only a fanciful though plausible interpretation, in the way of accommodation; but you cannot prove that such was the very precise meaning of the Parable, as given by the Holy Spirit."

I reply, it is very true, I cannot prove it directly and verbally as you require. For instance, I cannot produce any text which says in so many words, "*analogy is a reed, like unto a rod.*" But judging all Scripture by this concise rule, how many expositions, admitted by the above objector as conformable to divine truth, must be cut off! St. Paul says to the Philippians, "*beware of the concision.*" The same Apostle, after filling nearly half the eleventh chapter of the first of Corinthians with propositions of a spiritual nature respecting the difference between the man and the woman; which can neither be understood nor demonstrated, except by means of *the reed analogy;* foreseeing that they would be warmly disputed and contradicted by cavillers, says, "*but if any man seem to be contentious, we have no such custom, neither the churches of God.*" If St. Paul, therefore, despaired of convincing those who were full of the spirit of contention and contradiction, it will be high time for me to

tenwithin me, I knew not how (as described above by the Prophet Isaiah, but whom
I did not then know any thing of). I also traced
the whole progress of the soul and body (as
well as I was able to do) from infancy to
perfect maturity; showing that they were both
gradually increased and strengthened in a-
similar manner, till they were ripe and ready-
to fulfil the great object of God and nature, by-
entering respectively into the state of holy matrimony; from the affection of natural love in
one case, and divine love in the other; which
latter I considered as the spirit of God, which-
at this mature period operated, as I supposed,-
for this holy end, in all divinely instructed
souls, as the natural passion did, in all healthy
and well-nurtured bodies.

I little thought at that time, that the Holy
Scriptures, which I so wickedly and foolishly
despised, would have taught me the same things
(by the Holy Spirit) had I properly studied
them. But after my conversion (I hope) or at

desist. This I shall therefore do, after declaring my entire
persuasion, that perhaps there is not a mysterious passage in
the Bible, which may not, and will not in the Lord's good
time, be opened by means of this universal key; for HE
says, after interpreting the Parable of the Sower and Seed to
his disciples, " *For there is nothing hid, which shall not be*
" *manifested: neither was any thing kept secret, but that it*
" *should come abroad.*" Mark, iv.

least conviction of sin and righteousness, when
I had (almost miraculously) procured a Bible,
I read with a delightful surprise in St. Paul's
Epistle to the Ephesians the following Scripture,
and others of a like nature, which appeared to
me to teach the same truths, viz. " Till we all
" come in *the unity of the* FAITH *and of the* KNOW-
" LEDGE *of the Son of God, unto a perfect man;*
" unto the measure of the stature, of the fulness
" of Christ. That we henceforth be no more
" *children,* tossed to and fro, and carried about
" with every *wind of doctrine,* by the sleight of
" men, and cunning craftiness, whereby they
" lie in wait to deceive; but speaking the *truth*
" in *love, may grow up into him in all things,*
" *which is the* HEAD, *even* CHRIST ; *from* WHOM
" the whole BODY, *fitly joined together and com-*
" *pacted, by that which every joint supplieth,*
" *according to the effectual working in the mea-*
" *sure of every part, maketh increase of the*
" BODY UNTO THE EDIFYING OF ITSELF
" IN LOVE."

I also set forth in a way of comparison the
destructive nature of libertinism in the body,
with spiritual libertinism, or infidelity to God,
in the soul; the first as the shadow, the latter
as the substance; and proved clearly (to myself)
that the same causes induced them both, and
that they were equally and similarly fatal. That
the foul disease in the *body* was an exact

emblem of the similar corruption which took
place in the soul of the infidel, when it (scorn-
ing to submit to the lawful and holy matrimony
of truth and love, which I had discovered in
the soul, between right reason and true sentiment) went a whoring from truth, and the God
of truth, after the vain idols, the false pleasures of ambition, vanity, lust, covetousness,
&c. These I considered to be the painted,
tainted, and deceitful harlots of the soul, that
ruined mankind, by communicating the poison,
the infectious virus of infidelity, or spiritual
fornication, to the soul; which poison in both
cases attacked the source of life and generation,
and terminated both our natural and spiritual
life in corruption, and extinction of the vital
principles of faith and love.

 And now, the floods of light and heat, or
knowledge and faith, and (what I supposed to
be) divine beauty, which broke in upon my
mind and heart, on all sides, were infinitely too
copious, too rapid, and too spiritual, to be faithfully committed to paper ; for the views of
thought, and the ineffable feelings, which as it
were overwhelmed my soul with an ocean of ra-
vishing glory, wisdom, beauty, and holiness, in
the space of a few minutes, would, if verbally
and distinctly developed, have filled volumes! I
gasped for breath, I was continually ready to
shout aloud ; and when I attempted to write,
was unable to begin, from the boundless views

and transporting sentiments, which struggling in my soul, big with the mighty birth of heavenly. truth and salvation, rushed in crowds to be delivered! An invisible hand seemed to have with-drawn the veil from the face of nature, and for a moment to lay open all her secret treasures to my view. New languages in the various forms of matter entered the awakened eyes and ears of my soul, and revealed to me those spiritual realities, of which they were only the beautiful and eloquent (though silent) shadows.

Sometimes, I doubted whether I was not dreaming. I then brought my dreams to the standard of what I thought rational or mathematical demonstration ; and finding them to square, that is to say, as well as run parallel therewith (as it appeared to me), I concluded that I was awake. I then believed that I was, and must be, assisted by a supernatural power, and that the work which I was engaged in must undoubtedly be approved by the Deity, who thus vouchsafed to instruct and enlighten my blindness and weakness. Such a persuasion as this could not fail to stimulate my ardour; but at the same time, it threw a weighty impression of awe and reverence upon my soul, which made me more humble, tender, and cautious; which spiritually, as it were, made me to take my shoes from off my feet, being sensible that I stood on holy ground ; and rendered me exceedingly fearful, lest I should write any

thing discordant to truth, and to the infinite
holiness of that spirit, which I believed did
condescend to guide my utter weakness and
darkness.

   I concluded my Essay on the mutual resemblance of the soul and body, with taking a
general view of the brute creation, and showing
that all the good and evil sentiments in the
heart of man were strongly pourtrayed in
them; not only in their peculiar dispositions
and instincts, but also in the particular con-
formation of their bodies. That from observing
their natures and actions, man might learn
what was really good or bad, lovely or hateful
in himself; because all these several qualities,
actions, and forms had an appropriate voice,
and made their proper impressions on their corresponding originals in the human heart, and
excited concordant or discordant vibrations,
like those of two violins in unison, or the re-
verse; so that all impressions of moral evil or
deformity were immediately felt to be such, in
the pure heart*; by discordant vibrations, which
by causing uneasiness, or pain, self-evidently
proved them to be such, to its good natural
sentiments, and the same inversely.

---

* That is to say, comparatively, not absolutely; in
other words, a simple, unsophisticated, uncontaminated state
of the heart.

I also perceived that all discordant impres+
sions of deformity, whether natural or moral,
though painful at first, might in time cease gradually to be so, and even become pleasing, or
concordant; because that the first impressions
were always the strongest and clearest in point.
of contrast, and gave the greatest shock to
their opposites; and, that all subsequent impressions (if the first were not duly heeded)
became weaker and weaker, in proportion to
the frequency of their application. On the
other hand, I saw that the evil sentiments
of the heart, with which the deformed impressions were in unison (being as it were
roused and strengthened by sympathy) became.
continually stronger, in consequence of the
same general law of truth; which, like ALGE-
BRA, the type of that law, had a negative as
well as a positive efficacy and operation; so
that what weakened the good, nourished the
evil sentiments of the heart, to which they
were altogether congruous; until the most deformed and painful impressions should cease to
shock the good sentiments, which had by degrees either assimilated to them, or else were
extinct, as fire by water; by which means man,
if he neglected the warning of the first strong
shock, was carried away almost imperceptibly
from one extreme to the very opposite; for instance, from tenderness to cruelty; and was
wholly unable of himself to discover or effec-

tually to restrain his dangerous progress, unless
he had some fixed and original standard of right
and wrong to refer to continually.

I then attempted to demonstrate what was
evident to my own mind, that the laws of attraction and repulsion in matter, were real
ordained types and shadows of the laws of
moral and spiritual attractions and repulsions of
the heart; that is to say, of *desire* and *aversion*, with respect to good and evil, virtue and
vice, truth and error; and I supposed, that
probably the only difference in these seeming
parallels was this; that in brute matter these
laws were more fixed and regular, in appearance at least, because the law being once im-
pressed none could alter or suspend it, but the
Creator who first imposed it; but that man,
possessing, as I supposed, a certain inherent
power, or freedom of will, in himself, either to
obey the laws of right reason, or to reject them,
this inherent power, this *vis insita*, fixed by the
Deity in a being frail and mutable, eventually
gave rise to all the irregularities and eccen-
tricities which we observe in human conduct.

At the same time I did not feel certain in the
above theory, because I knew that there were
many and various deviations in matter, from the
general laws by which it was governed, which
proceeded from particular local causes; and my
own knowledge and experience, as well as my

reading, were by far too scanty to enable me to decide, whether or not these deviations in the natural system were as numerous and various as those in the moral. If they were, the parallel was complete and perfect.

I then became curious to discover how the dreadful power of evil could have acquired such a wonderful predominancy and absolute dominion in man, as it evidently possessed; for before this could happen, evil, I thought, must be in man as it were originally; else there could be no hold for its attractions, no sympathy therewith, but only antipathy, or aversion and repulsion *.

After numberless reflections upon the nature of good and evil, I came to this conclusion, *that God was, and must be, the one great source and perfection of GOODNESS and HAPPINESS. That His infinite happiness must be the necessary concomitant of his infinite goodness; and that all His rational creatures must approach towards Him in happiness in the exact proportion in which they approached towards*

* My reader will remember, that I am here only showing him what was the train of thought and argument which about thirty years ago led me by degrees to the belief of the truth. How far this argument was just, every man must judge for himself. I myself still think it was founded in truth *in general.* At the same time, I must except the temporary transient thought of original evil in man, which, however, quickly vanished when I came to consider the matter carefully.

*Him in goodness. I also saw and felt, that this
goodness must be voluntary; for* CHOICE *self-
evidently constituted its very essence, in the
nature of reason.*

Since therefore to be happy, that is, in order
to resemble God in this attribute, it was necessary that man should *choose* to resemble HIM in
goodness, it became requisite to place the
proper objects of this choice before him. This
choice then must be either of a kind of happiness similar to that of the Deity, consisting in
benevolence and all goodness; or of a kind of
happiness wholly different from that of the
Deity, consisting merely in sensual and selfish
gratifications. Now, the soul of man was
evidently enabled to make this choice, by being
for a time, during this life, confined in a fleshly
body, whose desires and appetites were wholly
opposite to those of the soul, being selfish and
sensual, while her's were benevolent and spiritual.

But still it remained to place such external
objects before this compound creature, as should
effectually excite, and stimulate into power and
action, the nature of both the parts of which
he was composed; that by an experience of the
pleasures and pains which belonged to, and resulted from each, he might, by the help of
right reason and just sentiment, be fully quali-
fied to compare them together, and finally de-

cide which of them was most calculated to make
him happy. If he preferred the happiness of
his soul, by choosing her proper objects, and
despising those of the body in comparison, it
was a manifest proof that he was capable of,
and fit to enjoy a happiness similar to that of
the Deity; which, I doubted not, would be conferred, after death had closed the trial. If, on
the contrary, he preferred the gratification of
his senses, to the happiness of his immortal
soul, it equally proved him to be incapable of
and unfit for a happiness resembling that of the
Deity; but as I then saw not the necessary cer-
tainty or justice of eternal punishment, which
appeared to me incompatible with the infinite
benevolence of God; I therefore concluded, that
such unhappy men, proving themselves to be
little more than brutes in a human form, would
be (and were) permitted, to enjoy, as they could,
the wretched lot which they had chosen, during
the term of mortal life; after which, being
utterly unfit for divine society, or any communication with God, which would only be torment to them, they would like other brutes be
annihilated.

Now, it was evident also, that such a system
of external objects, as I have mentioned as
necessary to the trial and choice of man, was
actually placed before him, in the whole world
in general, in the moral intercourse of men,

and very particularly in the brute creation. In
the tiger, and all ferocious savage animals, man
might read from his own right reason, and
just sentiments, or conscience, how detestable
cruelty, treachery, and all injustice, were to the
Deity, speaking to the soul, through the voice
of these witnesses. In the fox, and all the
tribes of little cunning, creeping thieves, he
might learn the baseness of cunning, deceit,
and fraud; in the goat and monkey he might
see the filthiness of uncleanness; and in the
swine of gluttony and drunkenness. On the
other hand, he might see and feel the beauty of
love and purity in the dove; of innocence in
the lamb, of honesty and industry in the ox,
and of humility and patience in the ass; and so
on. From all this I concluded, that virtue and
goodness consisted in the choice of such things
as resembled the moral nature of the Divinity,
in the manifestations of himself, which he had
graciously made in man by means of reason and
conscience; and that vice was the choice and
preference of such things as were manifestly discordant to the moral nature of the Deity, as declared by the same witnesses.

I then concluded from innumerable analogies, that the law of right reason, being fixed
and immutably proportionate, was shadowed
forth by the elements of *geometry*, as in Euclid's Elements; and that the unsearchable laws

of the imagination and heart, being altogether
variable, and fluctuating continually between
good and evil, were represented truly and accurately by the doctrine of *fluxions* and *attractions*;
and that the comprehensive and universal expressions of *algebra* were nothing more or less
than emblems of the respective natures and
relative operations of *good* and *evil*, *virtue* and
vice, *truth* and *falsehood*, which in like manner
were eternally *plus* and *minus* to each other.
That man was placed as it were in the centre,
between the *negative* and *positive scales*, which
might be expressed by two triangles, formed
by the intersection of two straight lines, their
equidistant bases being the extremes of good
and evil, and of course at the greatest distance
from each other; whilst man, at the point of
intersection, had both before him, and was
free to choose either the one or the other, being
in equilibrio*.

---

* The diagram imagined in the above paragraph may
possibly lead some reader to suppose I mean, that the two
triangles being equal, therefore the power of God in himself is only equal to that of the enemy. To obviate the
suspicion of such an idea *(impious and absurd)* I must
observe, that the latter is, I believe, in itself to the former,
as less than unity to infinite numbers. But yet, in the heart
of a wicked man, it is certain that the power of Satan is
much greater than that of God, in determining his conduct.
How then are these apparent contradictions to be recon-

All this appeared clear to me; but to make
it equally so to the world, would, I feared, even
from the little experience which I then had, be
an arduous task (though I saw not then a tenth
part of the difficulty, which, *without divine assistance*, appears *now* to me, like digging down
a mountain with a penknife). I therefore resolved
in the first place to take my Euclid, and try,
by comparison, how far the elements of natural
geometry did correspond to the law of the
rational mind. I therefore divided my subject
into three parallel heads and columns; the first

---

ciled? To this question (which, it seems, must come
from an unbeliever) I desire to reply, humbly and simply,
thus: the power of the Lord's grace in man (with reverence
I desire to speak, as a worm of the dust) extends not, I
believe, to absolute arbitrary force. HE does not, I believe, make men saints by absolute compulsion; for salvation is a free gift. In this way of coercion I humbly suppose HE could convert Satan, if it pleased HIM. HE
graciously places good and evil, life and death, before every
man, in the most effectual and sufficient manner, and then
permits him to make his choice; as Moses declares in
Deuteronomy, viz. " I call heaven and earth to record this
" day against you, that I have set before you *life* and
" *death, blessing* and *cursing*; therefore *choose life*, that both
" *thou* and *thy seed* may live." I therefore believe, that
the negative scale, or triangle, is as attractive to the flesh, as
the positive one is to the spirit; for the first contains carnal
things, and the latter spiritual things; so that the carnal
will be attracted by the carnal, and the spiritual by the
spiritual.

being common geometry; the second, I called
(as it appeared to me to be an idea of my own)
by the name of corpo-metry, including the
impressions of external objects on the human
body by means of the senses, and their effects
on the animal spirits; the third column, I
called ani-metry, regarding the internal laws or
reason, imagination, and sentiment, in respect
to the impressions made on the soul through
the medium of the body; also, that subsequent
arrangement of them under the heads of good
and evil, which we perform by the assistance of
reason and conscience.

I began with the consideration of *a point* in
each; to define which clearly, so as to preserve
any congruity with the definition of a point in
Simpson's Euclid, and at the same time to lay
a solid foundation for my figurative building,
I found to be the most difficult, or rather, the
most near to impossible of any part of my
work: because not only the kinds, but the
degrees of these points appeared to me innumerable; whereas the points of geometricians
have only one kind, and no degree at all, being
absolutely *nothing;* on which, therefore, their
whole system is built*.

* This consideration always brings to my recollection the
address of the Holy Spirit to carnal philosophers, in
Isaiah, xli. " *Produce your* CAUSE, *saith the Lord; bring*
"*forth your* STRONG REASONS, *saith the King of Jacob.*
" *Let them bring* THEM *forth, and show us what shall happen:*

But my mind expanding to my subject as I proceeded, I actually got through the whole of the definitions of the first book of Simpson's Euclid, in each column; very imperfectly, and in many respects very erroneously, no doubt; yet so much to my conviction and satisfaction, and in a manner that appeared to me so truly mathematical, or rational, that I had not a doubt remaining of the reality and general foundation in truth of my speculations; nor that I should be enabled gradually to disentangle, and arrange with sufficient clearness, the chaos of materials which I perceived in my mind, though as yet without form, and void of proper connection and regularity.

But I was here drawn aside from the straight line of this abstruse inquiry, into a collateral branch, which I slided into, through what I would call the capillary attraction of my wandering imagination.

"*Let them show the former things, what they be, that WE may* "*consider them, and know the latter end of them; or declare* "*US things for to come. Show the things that are to come* "*hereafter, that WE may know that ye are gods: yea, do* "*good, or do evil, that WE may be dismayed, and behold it* "*TOGETHER. Behold, ye are of NOTHING, and your work* "*of NOUGHT.*" This Scripture not only exposes the vanity of mere *carnal wisdom*, but also shows, to those who believe the divine inspiration of Isaiah, one or more beings, or persons, as co-agents with the Holy Spirit, on co-equal terms; a duality at least!

It was a matter of extreme surprise to me, to consider, that man being indued with right reason and lovely sentiments, according to the foregoing conditions; and placed between the two opposite attractions of good and evil (if the latter could be called such to a pure sinless being), with an equilibrium, or freedom of choice; and having also the Deity himself as the ultimatum, the infinite fountain of the attractions of goodness, to draw him to virtue, honour, happiness, and heaven! how it should, or could possibly so happen in practice, (as I was forced to own that it did, from my own woeful experience) that mankind, in part at least, should so wonderfully, so unaccountably prefer evil to good; and instead of being, as one would expect, drawn by the powerful and pleasant attractions of the Deity into the divine scale, more and more towards himself, should, on the contrary, be more strongly attracted towards the negative scale of carnal error; and dive as it were to such profound depths in it; plunging down, further and further, until the hour of death! What then could be the wonderfully powerful *source* and *principle* of evil, which could thus overcome in man all the demonstrations of the truth of reason, the attractions of the beauty of just and lovely sentiment, and of the Deity himself, the basis and the source of both?

.Had man, weak man, all this enormous
power and love of evil exclusively and originally in himself? This appeared to me to be
rationally and morally impossible; for man
was evidently a point in the centre, between
two opposite attractions, and did not (I supposed) stir, until he was first acted upon, from
one side or the other. There were indeed at
present, as I well knew, evil sentiments in man ;
and there was also, as I was equally convinced,
a perverted mode of reasoning; but to imagine
that these were implanted by the God of truth,
and that he thus fought against himself, was
equally absurd and blasphemous ; still therefore the principle and origin of evil, whatever
it was, which balanced, and sometimes out-
weighed, the influence of the Deity in our
hearts, was wanting to complete the system;
and this principle must necessarily be the exact
opposite of the Deity in all respects, and by
means of its powerful *negative* attractions *
and operations, incessantly maintain the empire
of darkness and error in man.

But though I could not find that evil was
originally in man, and much less that it could
be in the fountain of good, yet as the plain and

* The term *negative* is not here used in the common
acceptation. I do not mean only that it does not attract
in truth, but also that it *does* attract by error and falsehood.
My negatives are strictly algebraic.

obvious matter of fact was, that man thus
endued with right reason, and good sentiments,
and attracted by God through them, did still
break through this attraction, and rush wilfully,
though gradually, into extreme wickedness, far
below the baseness of mere brutal passion, it
became evident that man was deserving of proportionately greater punishment. For if a
brute was to be annihilated (as I supposed),
what, in the course of divine justice, was to
befal me and other wicked men?

This thunder-clap, so close, startled me
much, and following up the train of reflections
thus introduced, I was forced to see, that annihilation, which I had before allotted to wicked
men, as well as to mere brutes, was wholly
insufficient and inadequate to balance their
wilful corruptions in the scale of perfect justice.
The brutes truly, not being endowed with that
*divine reason and sentiment** bestowed by the
Deity on man, were not culpable with knowledge
of *good and evil,* with *knowledge* of *God,* and
therefore not in justice (I supposed) liable to
any thing further than annihilation, after the
ends for which they were made should be
answered: which ends, I supposed to be chiefly,
the instruction of man. But man, the son of

---

* " That was the true light, which lighteth every man
" that cometh into the world."—John, i.

God, could not act like a brute, without wil-. fully rebelling against the light of reason and sentiment, or conscience, and against God, whose witnesses and ambassadors they were; and it therefore became a mathematical or rational truth to my mind, that the punishment of wicked men after death might very possibly, or even probably, be almost eternal, considering the heinousness of their crime.

These speculations made me examine with more earnest attention, and an awakened suspicion, what the great evil principle of negative attraction, this perfect contrast and opposite to God, could be.

In the first place, it was not a mere brutal instinct, but, like the principle of *good*, was *intelligent;* for when man committed sin, it was known as sin. Conscience said, this is wicked, this will displease God; still, man persisted to sin, with the eyes of his mind open. Reason often said, the after pain will much exceed the present pleasure. This could not be denied, yet still man persisted to sin! But how could uncorrupt, innocent, sinless man act thus, without a stronger cause, an external evil cause? To do this, appeared quite contradictory, for it brought me back to evil originally in man.

Hence I became by degrees persuaded and convinced of the existence, *the personal ex-*

istence, of the great adversary of God and man, called *the devil,* whom for many years I had considered as a creature of the imagination only. I was at the same time forced to yield to the conviction, that evil, or sin, *was optional as such* in the author of it, and therefore could never cease to exist in that author. For God alone could destroy it by force, as I supposed; but his service was *optional,* from my premises; therefore, eternal justice and truth must eternally punish an eternal, wilful, optional sin.

From these considerations I was convinced to mathematical demonstration (of reason and faith) not only of the existence of the great adversary of God and man; but also, in the course of perfect justice and truth, of the eternity of his punishment; and lastly, by parity of reasoning, of the eternal punishment of those who resembled him in their wilful impenitence, and final perseverance in sin.

My reception of the above truths was not a little forwarded in my mind, by the study, as before mentioned, of geometrical figures, such as circles, squares, and triangles, with a reference to moral and spiritual truths. I perceived, that, as I had suspected, these figures had a secret and mysterious analogy with metaphysical subjects; and it was not without an emotion of horror and terror, that I seemed to discover, that Satan, the prince of darkness, must necessarily have his place in these schemes, in opposition, *diametrical* opposition, to the fountain of light, joy, and peace.

My eyes and ears, my mind and heart, were now widely opened with knowledge, to the awful view of eternity, which thus lay stretched before me, in perspective infinite of endless happiness and misery. The more I considered, the more I plainly felt and saw, that the great bulk, if not the whole of mankind, were on the brink of a perdition so deep, so inconceivably dreadful, that the mere reflection upon it seemed almost to petrify me. I saw, that if a stone would fall to the earth, so surely must the world, and all its vain pomp, descend into eternal perdition *.

I saw plainly, that after man once moved from the point of equilibrium, towards voluntary evil, he was in the course of divine truth

---

* That is to say, it appeared to me that the law of physical central gravitation, here alluded to, was nothing more or less than a strict type of the law of spiritual truth and just retribution; by which the soul that unreservedly obeyed the law of selfish, *or central* gratification, without regard to love, would be condignly punished by that very law! For *love*, as opposed to selfishness, is as the centrifugal to the centripetal power; and the latter, without the former, is a type of the next to omnipotent prison of the grave of hell.

already lost, as much, as if he had even reached
the source of it; because he could not do this,
without having previously and wilfully overcome
the power and attractions of right reason and
conscience, and of God; and being once thus
in motion in this spirit, the same mathematical
law of true retribution must 'carry him on,
willing or not willing, in the same crooked path
of error, with accelerated force and velocity,
according to the spaces of evil he moved through
in approaching to the centre of that principle,
like a descending projectile. It was therefore
clear, that if man once moved ever so little,
even a hair's breadth, towards voluntary evil,
he became utterly unable from that moment to
help, or stop himself, or prevent himself from
being drawn for ever towards the tremendous,
source of evil, which he had once wilfully inclined to and cordially obeyed.

Such being the case, I could see no remedy,
no possible way of salvation, except in the
grace and power of God. But how could these
in justice be either expected, asked, or given?
Every thing necessary, every thing possible, to
enable man to stand, except such an absolute
force as should destroy his equilibrium, or
freedom of choice, and consequently his re-
sponsibility, was given to him in the first instance, and nothing more could be given, if
we admit the necessity of a trial, or option.

Therefore, the justice and the goodness of God were fully established. But He was universally perfect, infinitely just, as well as gracious, and every attribute must be honoured. Who then was to satisfy his infinite justice and holiness, as well as his outarged goodness, thus wilfully and ungratefully insulted by rebellious man?

The story of *the creation*, and FALL of man, as recorded in the Scriptures, was now no longer ridiculed by me, as unjust, absurd, and even blasphemous; for I had actually, though without suspecting what I was about, or where I was going, fully demonstrated it (to myself) to be the very matter of fact; and not only fact, but perfectly holy, just, and good in God*. Because it was manifest that God, the principle and fountain of all good, being in himself perfectly good, could not have made man otherwise than good, and wholly free from evil, his antipathy; and it was equally evident that He had fully enabled man to remain so, if he chose, by gifting him with right reason and true sentiments. Hence it followed, that man's admission of evil was *a choice!* It was both premeditated and voluntary; for it must have discovered itself to be such, at its first approach

---

* That is to say, the grace of God's Holy Spirit demonstrated all this to me; but I thank God, I neither was, nor am, so brutish and blind in spirit, as to suppose that I made the discovery by my own mere wisdom.

feelingly to the *heart* and conscience, by the
violent shock which it must at first have given
to his just and lovely sentiments; and it must
have.been subsequently demonstrated to be so,
in the balance of right reason; and therefore,
the whole man, the *heart* and the *head*, the
woman and the *man*, having once committed
such an horrible act of rebellion against God,
with the eyes of the understanding open; he
had thereby, by his own free will and deed, delivered himself up, soul and body, to the lawful
sovereignty and dominion of evil, nd th
principle and god of it; and he had by the same
act equally renounced and thrown off his alle-
giance to the God of Truth, and consequently,
in perfect justice, forfeited his protection, and
incurred his high displeasure and wrath.

When this leading and important point was
established in my mind as an infallible truth,
I naturally was led to consider the nature
and possibility, or probability, of the Christian scheme of redemption through JESUS
CHRIST! that grand vital and fundamental
truth, which I had abused, despised, disbe-
lieved, and blasphemed, almost all my life.
Many weighty objections and obstacles to my
reception of this saving truth, were already removed; for I had proved already to my heart
and understanding (that is, the grace of God
had done it), though quite unexpectedly on

3

my part, all the previous and leading truths of revelation; such as the personal existence of *the devil,* the fall of man, and the probable eternity of his perdition; and I had also discovered, through the same agency, that God alone could redeem the lost race. Lastly, but first in importance, all the above valuable discoveries had been made to me, by the means of the dreadful torments of my merciful chastisements, which had driven out *the evil spirit of pride* which was the spirit of *blindness,* and *insensibility to divine truth, or the scales of Leviathan, as it is figuratively called in the Book of Job.*

But the difficulty lay here: how were infinite justice and holiness to be satisfied, without ruin to the sinner; eternal ruin? Since man had lost the power and the will, from the premises; since God alone could do this, how was He to do it? Could God freely pardon, nothing else being supposed, and re-establish man in his original situation? Would not man fall again and again? Could God improve upon his work by experience and repetition, like man? Impossible! I saw that there was a certain inviolable order in the nature of truth; and that if it could be broken through with impunity, the throne of God Himself would be overturned, and He would cease to be the Almighty!

Supposing then the Deity to have a Son,

according to the conditions of the Christian
faith, (which, though I did not understand it,
yet I was then fully disposed to believe, from a
sense of the omnipotence of God, and of my
own utter blindness, ignorance, and corrupt-
ness) supposing this to be the case, how far was
it possible, or probable, that such an exalted,
glorious, happy, and perfect being would condescend, by suffering for us, to pay the dreadful penalty which we had incurred; or that
His Almighty Father, against whom we had
sinned, would accept of such reparation and
satisfaction; nay, that He would even deign
(as it were) to be crucified in the person of His
Son, for the sake of such vile ungrateful creatures?

This appeared to me to be altogether so
astonishing, so incomprehensible! such a stu-
pendous height of love, mercy, compassion,
benevolence, generosity, magnanimity, if such
terms might be used in such a case ; and at the
same time (considering the infinite difficulty of
the arrangement, which was to reconcile such
contradictions and apparent impossibilities)
mixed with such infinite wisdom, holiness, and
justice, as entirely exceeded all bounds of human imagination! such indeed as no man could
approach to in thought, without infinite presumption and sacrilege, unless he knew God in
Christ. But as free and voluntary from God,

who alone had authority and power to make or
accept such an arrangement, I perceived at
once (by the gift of the grace of God, through
our Lord Jesus Christ) that this therefore was
God ; that this was the one very special reason
to faith, why it was not only possible, and
credible, but also must be absolutely certain.
It was what God alone could imagine, or con-
trive, or execute*!

† The above views of the Gospel salvation, though
lively, were yet only a few of the most obvious and striking
to me. I now consider, in addition, and to my higher
wonder, admiration, and adoration, that the Lord foresaw
that man would fall if He created him, and tried him as
He knew to be necessary and sufficient. Also, that He
knew that man must certainly perish eternally, if He,
HIMSELF, did not suffer the penalty of *death and hell*
for him. Also, that foreknowing all this, He still determined to create him, and to die for him, that he might live
for ever, and be partaker of His *own* nature and happiness; and that all the universe of angels and men might see
and know what was His real nature, and His ultimate will,
by means of what He *would* do and *suffer* voluntarily, as a
creature in our nature ; and *not only* by what He should
command His *creatures to do* and *to suffer*. That is to say,
that they might see and feel, that His real nature is *holiness and happiness; truth in love*. That by accepting a
vicarious sacrifice and atonement, they might see that His
indignation and hatred was against sin only, and not against
the miserable sinners of mankind. For he whose fierce anger
and just vengeance is personal, must sacrifice, must destroy
that person and *no other*. A vicarious sacrifice, if proposed
to such an one, must be an insult, as well as an absurdity.

It was the highest pinnacle of the divine goodness, power, and wisdom. I saw that He was indeed most glorious in all His mighty works; but I saw, and felt also, through grace, that all His other glories vanished away, as it were, before this *glory of glories*, miracle of miracles, holy of holies, so truly descriptive of His peculiar self, which is *love in truth*, and *truth in love*. I saw undeniably, that to worship Him in any other light than that of *redemption*, in any other character than in that of *the Father of our Lord Jesus Christ*, was to degrade His infinite majesty on one hand, and blasphemously to deny our own sin on the other; and lastly, to devote ourselves to eternal perdition.

Such rapturous thoughts and sentiments as these, rushing like lightning into my soul, fixed me down to my chair for a time, in a kind of stupor, or trance of mental abstraction, of

Lastly, to say no more, it becomes manifest from hence, that *all things*, even evil itself, is in the hands of Him, who " is *wonderful in council, and excellent in working ;*" (Isaiah.) —Even " *Glory, honour, and immortality.*"

Hence we may justly conclude, that if God has done and suffered so much for such a glorious purpose, and also for our particular benefit ; and if He has condescended to associate us in His labours, ought not man to desire to follow His example, and to co-operate a little, and suffer a little if necessary, in order to be not only a joint worker with Him, but also to share in His victory, honour, and eternal glory?

admiration and astonishment. Then suddenly
returning to myself, I started up, and running
over to the officer who was my sole companion
in this secluded situation, I informed him of
the surprising change which I had undergone in
the course of a few minutes, as it were, from
the most absolute and inveterate infidelity, to a
perfect belief of the Christian revelation, and all
its wonders.

This was matter of great surprise to him,
who was by profession a Christian, and had in
many previous conversations combated my
deistical sentiments, which I never attempted
to conceal from any man, because I was entirely
persuaded of their truth, and therefore could
not be ashamed of them. As this gentleman
was possessed of very amiable manners, we
had formed a rapid and pleasing intimacy,
which was particularly cherished by our situation; I had therefore shown him my speculations, as I committed them to paper, and he
had generally approved them as just in some
parts, and probable in others; but being un-
prepared by any geometrical knowledge, he
did not perceive all the force of my reasoning,
nor the exactness of my parallels; he was therefore of opinion, that I should not be able to
accomplish my object of proving the divinity
of morality and religion by mathematical demonstration, this appearing to him opposite

and repugnant to the will of the Deity, who
had left us all in some measure in darkness,
respecting such a mode of demonstration, in
order to prove our faith.

This objection, though not regarded at first,
did not fail subsequently to startle me, who
was then become more humble, cautious, and
fearful, from the proof which I had just received of my own extreme fallibility, blindness, and weakness, which had kept me during
so many years in chains of darkness. I also
then felt all my former wickedness, my impurities, and blasphemies with double force
and horror of heart; and thus dwelling more on
my own unworthiness, than upon the abundant
source of pardon, and comfort, and salvation
which I had just discovered, I became troubled
and agitated in a manner that I had not felt
before. I resolved in the first place, that I
would shut up my papers, and drop all such
speculations as those which I had for some time
followed with such intense ardour. I began to
think that it was impious and presumptuous for
a wretch like me, so full of all iniquity, to
pretend to inform or instruct others; and that
though the infinite mercy of God, through
Jesus Christ, had shown me the truth in such
a wonderful way, yet that my speculations being
formed and written in infidelity, they were un-
sanctified, and therefore wicked in themselves,

as well as highly dangerous; and for aught I
could tell, might be partly the suggestions of
the devil.

I then recollected my geometrico-meta-
physico speculations, my circles and triangles
of spiritual measurement, which had so strongly
assisted in morally demonstrating to me the
necessary existence, as I thought, of the evil
spirit. Ah! thought I, the stories which we
learn to ridicule of the enchanted circles of
witches, have then some foundation in truth,
and, perhaps, I am thus caught in the snares of
hell. At least I should most probably become
so, were I to continue to speculate on such
subjects. I have, with a daring but ignorant
hand, drawn aside the curtain which divides
the visible from the invisible world. I have
presumed to enter on the awful limits, and
who knows what I may meet there? No doubt
many miserable creatures, led on by a proud
profane curiosity, have thus been caught, and,
not being rescued by a special grace, have
perished for ever.

In all these reflections there was a mixture
of truth with error, which I was then unable to
discriminate; much less did I suspect that they
were the artful snares of this very enemy; who
finding that the cobweb labours of so many
years had been destroyed, and swept away, as
in an instant, by the infinite grace of my Re-

deemer, was not therefore discouraged or embarrassed; but, with peculiar art and address, shifted his mode of attack in a moment, to an opposite quarter; and knowing the confused, humbled, astonished, and timid state of my soul, assailed me immediately with all the terrors of superstition, and all the horrors of despair; hoping by this tempest, which he was raising in my imagination, to wash my feet from the rock on which my Saviour had just fixed me. But as the Lord was resolved to support, by His Almighty power, the gracious work which he had so mercifully begun in my soul; and as the strength, inveteracy, corruptions, and evil habits of my long apostacy, required unusual force of conviction to repress and subdue them, and to confirm my newly-acquired faith; so he was pleased to permit the adversary to assault me in a very severe, and, as I thought, uncommon manner (which, however, prudence forbids me to relate), that I might be fully convinced every way, both spiritually and naturally, how certain were those eternal truths which he had in infinite grace condescended to reveal to me.

I then found myself unable to return to my former studies; for my whole soul was filled with a variety of new and strange emotions, which I could not discriminate, nor controul. I only felt that I was become as it were a new

creature; that henceforth I had a new circle of
duties to perform, and of objects to contem-
plate; and I thought that the first thing necessary was to purge off my old stains, and purify
my heart by repentance, and prayers for pardon
and peace; not daring to believe that I was
already pardoned, and ignorantly supposing that
I must of course do something towards my own
justification.

About this time a circumstance occurred
to me, which might have a powerful tendency
to make my bodily organs assimilate with the
troubled state of my mind, and particularly my
nervous system, which appeared to be more immediately affected by this event; and as it certainly seems to have had this effect, and happened at so very critical a period, when it most
decidedly favoured the efforts of my spiritual
enemy to overwhelm me with fear, horror, and
despair; so I do not doubt in my own mind,
that it might be induced by him, and permitted
for wise and gracious purposes.

The situation that I was in, among the hills,
was in some respects very unhealthy, especially
to the natives; and I had no medical assistance
of any kind, which indeed I did not want for
myself or my companion; for the great exercise
that we took, and our airy quarters in the upper
fort, on the top of the hill, preserved us both
in vigorous health; but it was necessary for

many of the Sepoys, who were much troubled
with fevers, and agues, and obstinate sores,
which broke out chiefly in their legs and feet.
For all these cases there was no physician or
surgeon, except myself; but as it was my custom
always to carry with me, every where, bark,
James's Powders, Goulard's Extract, and Tartar
Emetic, so I dressed and administered to all of
them, to the best of my ability.

At this time then, one of my Sepoys had a
foul and obstinate ulcer in his foot; and he had,
as is common among the natives, by the power
of strong astringents, and such kind of ap-
plications, scarred it over at the surface, whilst
in the mean time (an emblem of their moral
state) the noxious matter had formed a sinus
beneath, and a collection of death the most
putrid and abominable. As I was not aware of
the consequences of suddenly opening such a
pit of corruption, I carelessly stooped down,
with my face directly over the part, and removed
the thin covering, which concealed all this
filth; but I had no sooner done this, than there
arose from the ulcer such a column of deadly
effluvia, and with such wonderful force, that it
seemed to penetrate even to my brain in an
instant, and by its subtle* and potent poison
wholly overpowered it, and took away my senses
for a few seconds. I was with great difficulty
able to stagger back into my chair, where I

* Figuratively speaking, but naturally subtil.

sat for some time, quite overpowered and almost insensible.

So soon as I came to myself I felt my nose, palate, and throat, to be tainted with the same abominations, which I plainly both smelt and tasted, to a degree that made me sick. I then called for vinegar, and applied it profusely to my nose and mouth, which might be of service to mitigate, but was unable to expel the poison, or prevent the mischief, which began and was completed in the same instant, as I apprehend; and I think that it probably did impart to the nervous fluid, or power, or organ (whichever physicians please), a deadly poison which clouded and disordered my natural brain; in the same manner and degree, as the spirit of legal fear and guilty horror from my enemy, did my intellectual sensorium.

If this matter be considered with attention, it will (or at least it may) appear, that the mischief which happened to my body, according to my belief, was an exact emblem of that which was offered to my mind; and it was also communicated in a manner perfectly similar. The object to be attained mentally, was to excite such a guilty fear and horror in my soul, from the sudden sense of my own wickedness, by *reflection** upon all my former impurities, abomi-

* This *mental* reflection is the action of the spiritual or intellectual brain upon the spiritual ulcer, and its deadly

nations, and blasphemies, as might overpower
my reason, which together with the faith of my
heart kept me close to my Saviour. The object
of the physical operation was to cloud, con-
taminate, and weaken the nervous energy of
my natural brain, the emblem of right reason,
and of our Lord Jesus Christ *, and through
it the strength of my natural heart, the seat
and source of faith and courage, by the similar
application of those corrupt and deadly effluvia
which arose upon the sudden opening of that
dangerous aggregation of putrid matter in the
natural ulcer.

Now, the ulcer, or rather the bottomless
pit, of my own heart's moral and spiritual corruptions and infidelities, had just been opened
in the same ignorant, unsuspecting way by
me (under a divine influence), and therefore,
through the medium of " *the prince of the power
" of the air*," as Satan is denominated by St.
Paul. The abominations which arose therefrom
were applied to my reason and conscience, in the
same violent rapid manner, and produced similar
effects proportionately, in the spiritual scale.

[*Five pages of the MS. are by advice omitted here.*]

matter; or which is the same thing inversely, the action of
the matter upon the brain; for $2 \times 3 = 3 \times 2$ and $2 + 3 = 3
+ 2$.

* Ephesians, iv. 15, 16.

When bed-time came, I desired to pray for pardon, peace, and protection; but when I attempted to kneel, I was opposed by I know not what spirit of dismal sullen pride, mixed with horror and despair; which painted me to myself in such colours, that I feared to present myself, a wretch fit only for hell, before the Divine Presence. Yet feeling that it was absolutely necessary, and that there was no time to be lost, I, as it were by main force, bent my stubborn knees to the earth; not free from a wicked shame, lest I should be detected in that humble posture; and raising my hands, remained for some time in that state, without daring to lift my eyes or thoughts to heaven, which appeared to me a presumptuous and vain effort. But at length, a fresh agony of horror and terror forced open my mouth, in broken ejaculations for mercy! Yet when I attempted to utter the words *Saviour! Jesus Christ!* I could not produce them. I was again opposed by a suggestion, that I did not believe in Him; that He knew this; that it was all mere pretence, extorted by fear, and that he would reject my impious hypocrisy! At last I exclaimed to this effect, "I do desire to believe in Thee, O Lord; I see the glory of this belief; I feel the beauty of Thy redemption, the necessity of it! O make me to believe; have mercy upon me,

K

miserable sinner! O save my soul from the powers of darkness!".

After some time passed in this manner, struggling against the desperate assaults of infidelity, guilt, and despair, I became more composed and calm, and resigned myself into the hands of my God and Saviour, with some degree of faith and hope. Yet I could not sleep; for a continual succession of gloomy ideas, heightened by the solitude and romantic wildness of the place, kept me waking. A tiger also that infested the hill, and broke the silence of the night with his hoarse voice, (which resembled the action of a large saw on a bar of iron,) appeared to my perturbed mind the messenger of the prince of darkness, whose vengeance he seemed to denounce against me (as he stopped at the foot of the wall, directly under my window), as a traitor and a deserter.

About this time, I had received orders to proceed to Bangalore, to take the command of the corps to which I belonged, it having become vacant by the death of the commanding officer; and I accordingly set off the next morning, the 3d or 4th of March, 1792, at daybreak.

[*Twenty-one pages of the original Narrative are here omitted by the advice of friends.*]

After my arrival at Bangalore, I became most anxious to procure a Bible, which I con-

sidered as the true bread of life, the true waters
of comfort, and the only effectual balm for my
wounded spirit. There appeared but little probability of getting such a book in such a place;
yet so great, so precious, were the mercies of
God to me, that after two or three days search,
he provided for me this inestimable treasure,
this pearl of great price, which I hardly dared to
hope for. This gift of God then became my great,
and almost only study ; and the more I read, the
more I was comforted, encouraged, and instructed
by its precious truths. I perceived the figurative
spirit, as well as the literal form, of all its
parts *; but when I came to read the Epistles of
St. Paul, my surprise was great, as well as my
joy, to find that the very things which I had
written at Ramghurry, respecting the resemblance of the visible and the invisible things of
God, and particularly the close analogy between
the human soul and body, and the symbol of a
spiritual matrimony in the union of man and
wife, were (as it appeared to me) all taught
therein ; only not in so detailed and essay-like
a manner, but with the authority, accuracy,
and concentration of the inspired Scriptures †.

* That is to say, in general ; not that I presume even
to think, that I understood one hundredth part of the particulars.

† See Romans, i. 19, 20 ; Ib. vii. ; 1 Cor. xi. 1—17 ;
Ephes. iv. 4. 12, 13, 14, 15, 16 ; Ib. v. 31, 32.

This *supposed* discovery * convinced me more fully, that I had been assisted in what I wrote, by the grace of God; who had thus by His Holy Spirit of Truth, through our Lord Jesus Christ, deigned to reveal to me in that secluded situation, the holy mysteries of his faith; and that these parts, at least, of my writings were not suggested by Satan. But though my faith was greatly confirmed by this coincidence, yet my adversary, and my own depravity, were still present to ensnare me, and by every means to turn truth into error, and error into truth, in my ignorant, weak, fearful, yet presumptuous heart and mind.

Happy and safe would it have been for me, *perhaps* (for I know nothing), had I, or could I have remained content in humble faith and practical knowledge, gradually acquired by obedience. What fiery trials and tribulations I should then have escaped! But my curiosity, my intense thirst for spiritual knowledge†, were so predominant; my heart and imagination were so ravished and transported with the beautiful

---

* I call it *supposed*, not because I have any doubts of its reality; that is impossible. But out of respect to the prejudices of those who are young in the analogy of faith.

† My present knowledge of the exclusive sense in which the word spiritual is used by evangelical persons, in England, makes it proper to say, that my meaning is more general; including evangelism, intellectuality, &c.

visions of divine things which I had already
seen, and which appeared to be daily discovered
to me, in reading the Holy Scriptures, and con-
templating the works of God in nature, that I
had in myself no power to stop.

On the other hand, I was strongly restrained
by doubt and fear, and by the recent recollection of the horrors of mind which I had just
passed through. This, therefore, was the proper
time for the enemy to endeavour to bewilder me
in the mazes of metaphysical speculation; and
at the same time, to make me suspicious of the
truth of my clue; and lastly, to make the distressing consequences of my want of faith
so many specious, though false arguments, for
my quitting the study of Scripture, nature, providence, and my own heart; a study to me so
full of thorns, snares, and pits. But the Lord,
I believe, only permitted the machinations of
my enemy to take place for my correction and
instruction. His gracious spirit, ever present
to preserve me, pointed out clearly all my errors
and absurdities, by their afflicting consequences,
both to my body and soul; and thereby taught
me gradually, how necessary it was to preserve
the medium line, and the right angle of moderation and truth, in every case *.

90

* That is to say, the right-angled triangle, or 45 ∆ 45
and the perpendicular, which divides the base into two equal

'The consequence of the superstitious errors and delusions into which I fell, was this, that I became continually tormented, alternately, by opposite persuasions and convictions, or spirits of belief and unbelief, whose struggles within me, rent my soul, and disordered my body. On one hand, the same lights of reason, and nature, and glow of sentiments, which *under God* had been the instruments of my conversion, and which I found to agree entirely with the truths of Holy Scripture, were still poured without my option into my soul *; and I both saw and felt, that they had every appearance of truth. But as I was so strongly prejudiced against them, through the artifices of my enemy, and feared that they might even be his own snares, I therefore endeavoured to resist their admission, and even to drive them out with all my might. This incessant and violent conflict almost overset my reason for a time. Its duration was long, and only yielded by slow degrees to repeated and severe experience, and the light of the law of perfect truth and liberty.

In consequence of the exhortations to tem-

_parts, are symbols of perfect moderation and freedom from all extremes; or, in other words, of perfect moral as well as natural truth.

* I confess, that the lights of reason and nature, without the teaching of the Holy Spirit, could not convert me; and I allow that the head may be convinced, without the conversion of the heart; but I pray for both.

perance in the New Testament, I resolved to be
more rigid and watchful over all my appetites;
and as the custom of smoking a hooka appeared
to me to be " *making provision for the flesh
to fulfil the lusts thereof,*" I determined, therefore, to relinquish this practice. I accordingly
did so, though with some difficulty and painful
effort, and left it off for about four months,
when necessity obliged me to resume it for my
health's sake. I also made it a rule, always to
prefer simple plain food in moderation; for I
argued, that the foods of the body being emblems of the foods of the soul, therefore all
rich pampering food was typical of pride and
vanity, &c. and gave to the body the same in-
flammatory temperament that the corresponding vices did to the soul. In this reasoning I
considered myself supported by the doctrine of
St. Paul; who says, " *Christ our passover is
" sacrificed for us ; therefore, let us keep the
" feast, not with old leaven, neither with the
" leaven of malice and wickedness ; but with the
" unleavened bread of sincerity and truth.*"
1 Cor. v. In the same manner I resolved
thenceforward to use wine only as a cordial,
to take only one kind, and in great moderation,
perhaps two glasses in the course of a week.

Had I stopped here, I should have avoided
many disagreeable and distressing events which
befel me; but then I should not have guined

the experience which was communicated to me
by those very events; and which taught me by
slow and painful degrees, that in man, the point
of moderation is the point of true wisdom; and
that this point is discovered to us only by the
practical knowledge of good and evil, in the
course of events.

It is worthy of observation, that I found
great benefit to my health from this regimen;
for though my bodily strength was not so great,
so audacious, so libertine as it were, yet my
appetite was always keen, and my stomach
clear; my intellect was also, I found, much
more quick and clear, in proportion to my temperance; and what was more valuable to me
than all the rest, the fires of the evil heart,
and the horrors of conscience, which I had
formerly suffered so severely, seemed to be
subdued, and to have lost their sting, which
consisted in the sense of guilt. But as I believed then, upon the best grounds, that I had
received pardon for all my past sins; so, through
this faith, the peace of God took possession
of my heart, and drove away the furies, the
harpies of hell, which had so long made it a
den of dragons.

As I have already observed, I struggled
hard to exclude from my mind all those internal as well as external visions of supposed
truth and beauty in nature, which were still

poured abundantly and involuntarily into my soul, and confirmed by the joint testimony of reason, imagination, and sentiment, as well as divine revelation; but the more I opposed them by argument, the stronger they became, and more self-evidently true to my conscience.

It was particularly in marching through large tracts of a beautiful country, diversified by mountains, fruitful valleys, extensive plains, rivers, and the distant ocean, that all these glorious witnesses for God, these silent eloquent parables of nature were explained with a wonderful clearness, and transporting beauty and harmony, to my soul*. They all spoke the language of moral and religious truth; in short, the language of the Holy Scriptures.

The lofty mountains which bounded the distant horizon, whose tops rose above the clouds, and whose bases were firm as the centre, which protected and fertilized the lowly vallies, reminded me of the power and manifestation of the Deity. But when I thought of exploring those heights without a guide, the fears of wild beasts, serpents, pits, rivers, quicksands, alligators, impervious jungles, &c. &c. all so fre-

---

* When the writer mentions *the soul*, he generally means the united mind and heart; which two appear to him to include reason, imagination, sentiment, or affection, memory, will, &c. &c, &c.

quent there, repressed the rash conception.
Then the natural association of my ideas led
me immediately to the rashness and presumption of deists, or natural religion men; who
think to find God, by the unassisted eye of
human reason.

In passing through thick jungles, full of
thorns and briars, poisons, and wild fruits,
blended together; abounding with game, and
also with beasts of prey, and venemous serpents,
scorpions, &c. I beheld in them a lively picture
of the world and all its vanities and snares.
In the thorns, I saw those over-anxious cares
for the good things of this life, which render
men selfish and ready to tear one another to
pieces, and to snatch something from every
one who comes within their reach. In those
whose thorns curved inwards, and therefore
admitted an ingress, but caught fast hold of
those who attempted to retreat, I saw the
dangerous nature of worldly pursuits, and
worldly society; which freely admitted all
comers, and only caused their hooks to be
felt, when the palled appetite perceived their
bitterness, as well as vanity, and experience
warned us to retire. Others, whose blossoms
emitted an aromatic, enlivening, or sweet
fragrance, and whose straight thorns pointed
outwards, appeared to be emblematic of more
specious, honourable, and intellectual objects,

which cannot be attained without pain and
difficulty, but which, nevertheless, bear no vital
fruits: such are the mere human sciences.

The narrowness, curvedness, and multipli-
city of the paths made through these woods,
by the foot of curiosity, or uncertainty, or
caprice, or imaginary brevity, pointed out the
various opinions of men, in their search after
happiness, through the great wilderness of
human life.

The extremely narrow limits of the prospect, bounded on all sides by the surrounding
thorns, showed me the equal shortsightedness
of those who are the mere men of this world,
and have no object in their mind's eye, beyond
the vain and selfish cares of this life.

The game, so plentiful and various in the
depths of the wilderness, and so alluring to
young sportsmen, pointed out the painted pleasures of the world, which are so tempting to
youth, and seduce them without reflection so
far into the entanglements of the labyrinth, that
they are sometimes lost for ever in mazes of
error, or in deep pits; or seized, while intent on
their sport, by the royal tiger, the king of the
wilderness of this world; or perhaps poisoned
by the specious, high coloured, but fatal fruits
of infidelity and false doctrine, which abound
therein.

When, on the other hand, I emerged from

those jungles, and entered into an extensive
plain, where the distant horizon was terminated only by the bending skies, I found
my own mind expanding in the same manner;
and the very reflections which were introduced
by the objects before me, showed plainly, in
the course of a little comparison and arrangement, what they were ordained to typify, or
figure forth.

Thus, when men tired of the vain pursuits,
cares, and pleasures of the world, retire for a
while into the wide plains of meditation and
speculative comparison, their intellectual sphere
of vision becomes proportionately enlarged, and
is terminated only by the distant view of another world. As they recede farther and farther
in thought, from this world, its vanities, which,
when they were close at hand, appeared so
important and filled their mind's eye, vanish
successively into dark, confused, and uninteresting points, which appear all nearly alike, which
by their quick recession display their very
trifling extent, until the whole mass shortly
appears as one indistinct, uninteresting blot of
blackness. By a comparison of this with the
remote objects, upon the verge of the horizon,
and of human existence, which gradually en-
large and open to our view, we discover their
relative magnitudes and importance, and learn
to make a true estimate of all worldly objects.

Hence I perceived that mankind, particularly
such of them as lived altogether to, and in the
world, calculated the value of all objects,
not by their real, but by their apparent bulk,
as seen from the centre of the picture of human
life, through the medium of the eye of self-
love; that is to say, by their nearness to, or
remoteness from, the centre of their own hearts'
interest, or pleasure; that is to say, the interest
or pleasure of their own hearts. Thus, to a man
in a jungle, the bramble bush that fills his eye, is
an object of much greater apparent magnitude
than the sun, from the rays of whose piercing
heat and light he takes shelter under his bush.
Thus also, to a man plunged in selfish cares,
the pitiful object close to him, which occupies
his whole thoughts, or mental eye, is of more
importance than the eye of heaven, from the
piercing rays of whose convictions in his conscience, he takes a temporary refuge in his
worldly business. Hence I saw, that in abstract speculation, mankind made use of the
immutable laws of *geometry,* or *right reason;*
but that in practice they were necessarily di-
rected by the specious, but deceitful rules of a
perspective arbitrary, and continually changing
with the situation of the spectators, who made
their own eye the centre of the picture; that is
to say, made the magical delusions of inordinate self-love, the standard of good and evil,
of true and false, of great and small, of near

and remote; and which delusions the flatteries of the old serpent, acting upon their carnal minds and hearts, made them unable to discover, or even to suspect.

This again pointed out in the clearest manner, the insufficiency of the human eye, or human carnal reason, to guide us safely through life, and to salvation; for though we perhaps may sometimes reason rightly, when we reason *abstractedly* or geometrically, yet the moment we come to act, the opposite scale of our neighbour's good, which ought to balance our own, is imperceptibly dropped and lost sight of in the mists of the heart, raised by the heat of passion*, from a subtilized imagination.

From these reflections of natural things into the mirror of the eye of my mind, I saw plainly, that the *heart* and *imagination* were artists of superior genius, consummate landscape painters, whose colours were most vivid and glowing, whose lights and shades were so disposed as to give an effect much beyond the common course

---

* Though the figure is somewhat changed here, yet the moral deduction is precisely the same, as that of actual distance; for actual distance from the eye, means moral distance from carnal reason, or self-love; which by diminishing the angle under which the object is seen, does apparently diminish its magnitude or value; for moral magnitude is value or importance. Hence, it is demonstrated, that every thought, word, and deed of the natural man, in moral life, is false.

of nature; and whose perspective was perfectly correct, according to the rules of inordinate self-love, or *falsehood*; diminishing all objects, as they lay more distant from this central point of self. . I saw that the whole world was enchanted by the pleasing sorceries of these cunning witches, who carefully preserved the delusions of moral perspective in all their pieces; and that all men greedily bought their specious and fascinating, but dangerous delusions.

.: On the other hand I saw, that right reason, founded on divine truth, was a studious, sober, accurate delineator of charts and maps; in which every object was represented according to its real comparative magnitude and situation, and in its proper *latitude* and *longitude*, or *morality* and *religion**; and that one of the least of those faithful plans was of more value than an hundred of the deceitful lies, of the landscape painters, or romance writers. But as these useful charts wanted the high but

---

* *Latitude* is truly emblematic of *morality*, and *longitude* of *religious truth ;* because the sun is a *shadow* of divine truth and love, and the earth is an emblem of man. Hence the dominion of religion (whether true or false) is from the rising to the setting *of the sun ;* and the extent of morality is from the north of self-love to the south of social love, whether the true or the false, from *Poles* to *Equator*. Morality is ascertained simply, by an equal balance, or meridian observation, " thou shalt love thy neighbour as thyself." But to discover the true longitude of true religion, is a much more difficult task.

false colouring, the striking effects of exaggerated
light and shade, the seducing imagery, and
flattering perspective of the landscapes; so no
one admired, few understood, and none purchased them, except a few *navigators* or *geogra-
phers*, for purposes of mere utility*. From these
causes it necessarily followed, that right reason
was suffered to starve, and the Bible to moulder,
for want of employment; whilst the two deceitful, vain painters, the spiritual adulterer,
and whore, were lodged in palaces, and universally adored as idols and prophets.

When we came to cross rivers, I again saw
the necessity of a faithful and skilful guide at
every step, to point out the proper *fords*, and
to mark the *quicksands*, which often lay thick
on each side, and caught those whose rashness,
obstinacy, and self-conceit, despised wholesome
caution, and chose to take a bye path of their
own. Also, to discriminate the shallow from
the deep waters (of doctrine) which would
overwhelm the ignorant and presumptuous;
and to point out the sands and rocks of offence.

All this was a sermon to me in the genuine
language of nature, which I was enabled to
translate, and which I found to be truly Chris-
tian-like; and it all tended to this one point, or

* Navigation is the emblem of metaphysics, and geo-
graphy is the emblem of moral philosophy; as astronomy is
of religion, or the science of the heavens.

4

centre *(not focus*)* of truth, viz. that fallen
man was utterly blind and feeble in himself,
and yet surrounded on all sides by inevitable
snares, and insurmountable obstacles, in the
road to eternal life and happiness; and that,
therefore, it was downright insanity, for such
a worm, blind as he was in himself to spiritual
truth, to determine to grope out his dangerous
way through all these obstacles, by his own
proper wisdom and power.

Thus every object in nature was to me a
parable full of instruction; but my notice was
more particularly atttracted by the animal
creation; amongst which " *the villain spider,*"
as Thomson calls him, arrested my attention
in the most forcible manner. This loathsome
insect always, but then more particularly, appeared to me to be a strong and admirable emblem in miniature of my great adversary, " *the
lord of flies, Beelzebub.*" His extreme quick-
ness of sight, and feeling, his continual watch-
fulness, profound dissimulation, and patient
lying in wait; his cunning, fierceness, and
cruelty, his rapid motions, strength and ac-
tivity†; his powers of titillation as well as of

---

* As circular, and spherical, square and cubic geometry,
is symbolical of right reason, and divine truth; so conic
sections, and all oblique and elliptical measurements and
movements, are emblematic of error and falsehood.

† Spiders in *India* are different things from what they

strongly seizing, in his long legs, with which
he appears to tickle his violent captives, and
makes them whirl round, while he folds them
in the shroud of death, spun out of his own
bowels. Also, the beauty, regularity, and elas-
tic force, of his *mathematical snares ;* some of
which, viz. those suspended in gardens, have
the form of the hexagon, and equilateral triangle*, or are circles so divided by radii, which
are joined all round by parallel lines that form
so many distinct and concentric polygons ! How
fine and fluctuating, yet how strong and sure,
are these snares, in which poor silly flies, so
sportive, thoughtless, and wanton, so much
like human flies, are continually caught ! Another very striking analogy in the natural his-

are *in England.* In India their bulk, strength, activity, and
boldness are wonderful, and almost incredible, as well as
their venom.

* The equilateral triangle, or chord of 120°, and the
hexagon, or chord of 60°, are, in my Essay on the analogies
of geometry, shown to be emblems of *the letter of the law*
without the Spirit. It is in this snare, as in a cobweb, that
the devil catches the souls of men ; for the letter being only
equal to the *radius*, whilst the spirit of it is equal to the
sinus totus, or *chord of* 90, they are enabled for a time to
conform to the letter, (as legal hypocrites) externally, until
they are tempted to transgress the letter openly, which
being felonious, they are hanged. Thus " the letter killeth,
but the spirit giveth life," for " the Lord and His Gospel are
that Spirit."—2 Cor. iii.

tory of spiders and flies, is this: the latter are very fond of the light, and continually endeavouring to approach to it; on which account the crafty spiders generally spread their nets in the windows, by which policy they catch multitudes of those insects. It is evident, that the human flies who are so fond of the light are natural philosophers, and those of the infidel order, are therefore continually entangled in the snares of the lord of flies, whilst vainly seeking for light in nature, whereby they may attain to perfect and unbounded liberty.

All these reflections, and many more which continually rushed into my mind upon the sight of every natural object, appeared to me to be so applicable, and upon the whole so rational, as well as beautiful, and corresponded so entirely with the truths of divine revelation, or the parables of Holy Scripture, that I could not, in my lucid intervals, refuse to believe them. But as I was, on the other hand, extremely fearful of the blindness and fallibility of my own understanding, and conscious of the narrow limits of my own knowledge; and as I dreaded, and even magnified by a faithless fear, the wonderful powers of delusion and seduction of my enemy; so I resolved by no means to dwell too much upon, or regularly to investigate, these curious things, lest I should fall at unawares into his snares as before; for

though they were certainly true in themselves,
yet if they were suggested by him I saw plainly
that it must be for some evil purpose of pride
and eventual impiety. If, on the other hand,
these beautiful visions were afforded by the
grace of my Saviour, I was confident that he
would in due time clearly demonstrate to me
that they were so. I therefore determined to
decide upon nothing, but to wait patiently, and
apply myself continually to the study of the
Scriptures; which alone were to be depended
on, as the source and standard of divine truth.

In the course of my close application to the
study of the Scriptures, I necessarily met with
many parts, which I could not properly digest
or understand. Indeed, such was my timidity,
and self-diffidence, and fear of my enemy, that
I hardly ever ventured to think or reason freely
on any difficult text; but resolved, as the safest
way to take, and if possible, to obey them all
literally. Observing that our Saviour cast out
a spirit of lunacy which His disciples were
unable to do, and that one cause assigned for
it was this, viz. " *Howbeit this kind goeth not*
" *out, but by prayer and fasting*," I became
strongly inclined to think, from the uncom-
monly agitated state of my mind, which, like
the ocean vexed with fierce winds, never rested
day or night, that I was possessed by such a
spirit. And truly, the incessant struggles

within me, between faith and fear, did to a poor blind worm render such an opinion very plausible. However, I resolved at all events, if there was such a spirit in me, to drive him out, since the mode was clearly laid down by our Lord himself. I therefore, after praying for a blessing upon my weak endeavours, immediately entered upon a course of severe fasting and continual prayer*.

* I have since heard a new exposition of the above text of Scripture, viz. *That it is not the diseased and possessed person who is expected to fast or to pray for himself; but the priest or exorcist, who is to fast and pray for him.* I confess, that this opinion does not appear to me to be very probable, except in as much as it regards the prayer. Prayer must no doubt be necessary, and the poor lunatic cannot (except in a lucid interval) be expected to pray for himself; therefore the exorcist must undoubtedly pray, and with real genuine faith too, in order to succeed. But how can the fasting of the priest benefit the lunatic? It can only be by *miracle*, and the reception of such doctrine would evidently carry us back to the dark ages of popish superstition and imposture. I therefore apprehend, that the lunatic must fast, or *be made to fast,* for himself. He cannot be made to pray, but he may be made to fast. Exclusive of these considerations, there is a natural tendency and fitness in fasting, to cure, or at least to mitigate all such kinds of disorders; of which certain fits seem to be a species.

I have known more than one person visited by fits, very similar in appearance to those described in the Gospel concerning the lunatic, who were much relieved, and one positively cured, during the period of his abstinence from wine,

For about a fortnight, I ate little besides bread and water, in small quantities; and twice in every week I fasted altogether for one day, and the first time for two entire days, or forty-eight hours. I also passed the whole of each day, from sunrise till sunset (excepting only the unfrequent calls of subaltern duty) in earnest prayer, reading, and meditation, on my knees, or on my feet; with the exception only of such intervals of rest, as were absolutely necessary to keep me from fainting with heat; and observing that David says, " At midnight will I rise," &c. I also arose and prayed often when I awoke during the night.

But I did not succeed so well, as I had expected by this rigorous regimen; for I found that hunger often made me fretful and impatient; and I also found my strength much diminished, and that I was no longer able to do my duty properly. Also, my hunger often became so urgent, that when food was before me I could not restrain myself, when once I began

spirits, smoking, and *much* animal food; that is to say, one year. After this he resumed his old habits, in consequence of which his fits returned immediately, with increased violence.

The state of intoxication and heat, into which the mind as well as body is thrown by such excesses, seems to rouse the evil spirit, and to be a kind of signal, that he may lawfully attack the backsliding sinner.

to eat, but often ate so immoderately, as to hurt my health by the contrast between entire emptiness and repletion.

Yet mistaken as I was, I do believe that my blind endeavours were graciously accepted, because they were sincerely intended in humble faith; or rather, the Lord, having called me unto eternal life, was pleased to excuse my follies and infirmities for his covenant's sake. Neither were they useless; for though I perceived no sensible expulsion of any evil spirit, yet the inconveniences that resulted from my errors, taught me, by slow degrees, that MODERATION, or TEMPERANCE, was, in the course of nature and Providence, the point of perfection in the worm man; and that every degree beyond this right angle, and true perpendicular, only carried him nearer to the regions of superstition on one side, or of sensuality and licentiousness on the other.

In my silly misapplication of truth, and true principles, I preferred to eat *unleavened bread,* though it did not agree with me, because it was an emblem of " *sincerity and truth ;*" and though milk agreed still worse with my stomach, yet I used it as a meal, because St. Peter terms the first principles of the Gospel " *the sincere* " *milk of the word.*" Not that I thought there was any *holiness* in milk, but I thought that it must be particularly nourishing to obtain the honour of being such an emblem.

The longer I persisted in this very foolish regimen, the more enfeebled I became in mind and body; till at last a sudden instinctive sensation, like the voice of expiring common sense, told me that I was acting most absurdly, and that my health and strength would be immediately restored by a change of diet, and a moderate use of the hooka, or Indian pipe.

I resisted this impulse for some time, as a snare and temptation of the devil; but as it became daily more powerful, and my weakness more intolerable, I at last (after consulting by letter an old staunch Christian at Madras, for whose opinion I had a high respect, and being assured by him that there could be no harm in it, if taken in moderation) resumed it, after first beseeching the Lord to sanctify it to me, and to pardon me if I was doing wrong. The consequence of this was, that the very first day I used it, I got such bodily strength and comfort, as to be able to take a walk of three or four miles, without inconvenience; in two or three days my disorder was stopped, my stomach digested its food, which I changed from milk to flesh, and I recovered my health and animal spirits.

From this circumstance, I hoped that what I had done was not criminal, since such a

blessing had followed it (if indeed any thing
could properly be esteemed a blessing, which
nourished my sinful body*, of which I still
doubted); and as my Christian friend told me,
that there was no end to these vain scruples,
and that the religion of Christ was a religion
of freedom and reason, I therefore began to
think that it might also be lawful for me to resume the study of the various analogies between the visible and invisible worlds. I now
believe that I was right, and that nothing made
it hurtful to me but this, that I soon began
again to doubt whether it was not sinful; and
this doubt gave the devil every opportunity that

* My reasonings on this subject were curious; and being
partly true, were therefore more dangerous. I said in my
heart, *I am born in sin, and by nature a child of wrath, and
whatever I do naturally is therefore sinful. Above all, my
natural body is a lump of sin and death ; whenever I gratify
it beyond the absolute necessity of supporting life, I commit
sin, although I hope I am converted; and whenever I deny
and mortify, and crucify it, I please God. O that it were
lawful to kill this cursed body at once, and enter into life!
But no, that must not be. I am required to be a living sacrifice, and to become holy and meet for glory, in the course of
a life of constant crucifixion, like our blessed Lord and
Master! But how shall I hold out under such continual
misery?* "O wretched man that I am, who shall deliver me
"from the body of this death? none can do it but God,
"through Jesus Christ our Lord." Amen, so be it. I forgot
that we are to be "temperate in all things."

Scripture, not only what I had formerly meditated for the good of the world, but much
more; even of demonstrating not only the
truths of natural religion, but also those of
the everlasting Gospel, in the most geometrical
manner *. Yet such an undertaking still appeared too high, too presumptuous for me; and
I was still apprehensive that such an attempt
might have dangerous consequences. What
those consequences might be I was not exactly
aware; but at all events, I feared that many
would continue to disbelieve after all that I
could say; and therefore, that their condemna-
tion must be so much the greater for rejecting
such strong proofs. This fear, which I could
not then surmount, made me resolve not to
venture upon any thing of the kind; yet as it
appeared to me that a narrative of my own
conversion would be a proper medium line;
that it might be of great service, in displaying
the dangers of infidelity; and also tend highly
to prove, in a practical manner, the divine truth
of Christianity, in all its parts; so I concluded,
that this at least was lawful and right, and my
duty.

* Here I confounded the great commandments of the
law, as promulgated by our Lord, with the peculiar truths
of His Gospel; but the first are *only absolute truth*, the
latter are " *grace and truth.*"

This therefore I resolved to do, and therein employ my leisure time; which, as I lived wholly secluded from society, dreading it as much, and perhaps, even more than I dreaded myself, was great, and often hung heavy on my hands.

It nevertheless occurred to me subsequently, that it was my duty to confess my Saviour before men, and to endeavour to win lost sinners to Him, by a relation of the wonderful things that He had done for me. I therefore began to relax from the strictness of my solitude, and to dine abroad sometimes; always taking care to return thanks aloud before all the company, to their great surprise and amusement! It was no wonder; for neither they nor I had ever seen such a thing done before, at least since the period of my arrival in India.

After continuing this new practice for some time, together with a corresponding "demeanour" of general conversation; always ready to answer for myself, and give a reason of the hope that was in me; I found that I had not made any perceptible progress towards the conversion of a single individual. I only found that some pitied me and advised me to abandon these follies, or I should be lost and ruined; that others despised and laughed at me as a crazy weak-minded creature; and that others thought me likely to be a more serious disturber of the

peace of society, in short, a proud, presumptuous, conceited enthusiast. Not a few had
sagacity enough to see that I could not be
shaken by their arguments, whose chief force
lay in ridicule, which I did not feel. They,
therefore, attacked me through the medium of
the palate, with a show of hospitality; and I
suffered considerably by this manœuvre, through
a desire to avoid singularity and preciseness,
before I perceived all the danger that I ran.
The general conversation also was of a description most shocking to my lately-acquired
sentiments, and often seemed to be levelled at
me. At last I resolved to withdraw myself
again from society, since I could do no good in
it, and endeavour to make up for this inability
by my solitary occupations.

This indeed was infinitely more agreeable to
me; for I never went into company without
horror and dread, on account of the lewdness
and impiety which continually shocked me;
but at home I conversed with nature, and
through the medium of the Scriptures with my
Saviour, who poured wonderful comforts of
faith, hope, and love into my grieved heart, by
the grace of His Holy Spirit, which made the
emptiness of worldly pleasures to appear like a
dunghill to me. I desisted therefore from my
vain attempts at conversion; and applied myself
exclusively to the study of the Scriptures, the

instructive parables of God in nature, and the narrative of my own reformation." Yet I found it difficult to do this, without making frequent use of analogy in the way of illustration; for as these natural parables would rush unbidden into my mind, with tempting solicitation, on such occasions; so I could not always overcome the desire. I felt, to assist my own weakness with their power.

At first, I was very reserved and cautious; but by degrees, I became more bold and free, and at last too much so for the state of my feeble mind, and little faith; hence the saying of St. Paul was again verified to me; viz. "*He that* "*doubteth is damned (or condemned) if he eat* "*because he eateth not of faith; for whatsoever* "*is not of faith is sin.*"

I was, therefore, suddenly assaulted with such *floods of dreadful thoughts,* as over-whelmed *my reason* in a moment. In short, the *gulfs of perdition* seemed to open be-fore me at every step, and I was almost drowned in *the great metaphysical deep!* Then I felt, and thought I understood something of the following texts: "*When He raiseth up*

Eating and *drinking* are emblems of *redding, hearing,* and *thinking.* Therefore in Scripture men are said to eat and digest books. Also Solomon gives directions for eating HONEY.

" *himself, the mighty are afraid; by reason of*
" BREAKINGS," *(of the sword of reason)* " *they*
" *purify themselves. The* SWORD *of him, that*
" *layeth at him, cannot hold, the* SPEAR, *the*
" DART, *nor the* HABERGEON. *He maketh* THE
" DEEP *to boil like a pot; He maketh* THE SEA
" *like a pot of ointment. He is a* KING *over*
" *all* THE CHILDREN OF PRIDE."—Job, xli. See
description of Leviathan.

I then became more fully persuaded of the
presumptuous and impious tendency of the
things that I was writing, and that they exposed
me to the assaults of Satan; I therefore again
burnt the whole of what I had written, with a
resolution never again to venture to speculate
upon such high and deep subjects, which I
found to be as it were guarded by cherubim
with a flaming sword that turned every way,
to keep me off from the tree of knowledge;
which sometimes appeared to me to be the tree
of life, and sometimes of death, according to
the strength or weakness of my faith.

This was a very dangerous situation, and
must have been fatal, the devil urging me behind, had I not been protected and supported
to the last by my most gracious Lord.

In the first place, what was I to do? The
study of Scripture I could not pursue exclusively and perpetually; besides, it was too
nearly connected with reason and nature, by

means of analogy, and therefore appeared to be
to me a snare; and all profane books and studies
seemed equally dangerous. Exhausted at last
by fruitless conjectures, and search after something that I might venture to do without the
fear of being damned, I began to lose all patience; my brain seemed to burn; and my heart,
rent with agony, wished for the asylum of death.

Downright necessity of self-preservation
drove me at length to do what I so much
dreaded; that is to say, to apply to be admitted
into the general mess of the corps, from which
I had hitherto kept myself separate. I was accordingly admitted with much kindness; for
hopes were again formed of me, as of one returning again to common sense and to the world,
from the temporary attractions and degrading
shackles of a dismal and antisocial superstition.

To complete as soon as possible my deliverance from the horrors which had fastened on
my mind, as the natural and judicial consequences of my faithless folly, I resolved to read
some light, entertaining book, which might
divert my spirit; I therefore wisely took up
the Arabian Nights Entertainments. But I
here experienced a severe reproof and chastisement for my folly. The enemy was immediately permitted to suggest such tremendous,
detestable, unutterable impieties and blasphemies to my imagination, that I suddenly started

M

up, and, throwing away the book, I ran out of
my tent in a transport of horror, terror, and
almost desperation. I then ran in again, not
knowing how to escape from myself, and quite
distracted for a time. Then, as the last resource, I betook myself to prayer; but the same
horrors presenting themselves, even then, I was
forced to stop short through fear, lest the wrath
of heaven should strike me in an instant to
hell, for daring to offer a sacrifice so full of
pollution and abomination.

I was then quite confounded and at a loss
what to do. I was driven, hunted by my enemy,
and by my own folly, to the last extremity of
the mazes of my absurdity, and must either
perish in his nets, or break through them. I
fell into a debate within myself whether I was
a redeemed one, or not; and I began to think
that it would be best to die at once, to prevent
more horrible sin.

But here it suddenly and mercifully occurred
to me, that I had already been preserved in a
situation the most fearful, and seemingly
perilous, that a human being could be placed in
at Bangalore; and that, therefore, to despair
after this, would be the height of folly and infidelity. I then instantly suspected that all
these horrors must be mere tricks, snares of my
enemy, to terrify and drive me either to despair
and suicide, or to renounce a religion so full of
vexations and torments, *to me.*

In consequence of these reflections, I became more composed ; and, justly believing that this discovery had been made to me by the mercy and compassion, in wisdom, of my Saviour, I was filled with gratitude, and returned sincere thanks for this gracious, though dear-bought experience.

By the help of the knowledge which I had thus gained of the devices of Satan, and the faith which it gave me, I combated these horrors of blasphemy day and night; (for they became incessant, and kept me awake and literally sweating with misery and horror, almost the whole nights through) and I learnt to make it a rule, whenever they assaulted me, to betake myself to prayer and praise, and to read, or repeat by heart, some of David's beautiful Psalms. My enemy, therefore, finding himself discovered, and that he only drove me *to*, instead of *from* my Saviour, by his *fiery darts*, and *swords*, or " *bitter words*," desisted by degrees; and in the course of a month or two, they were (God be thanked!) quite overcome or discontinued.

All these fiery trials tended ultimately to increase and strengthen my faith, patience, and knowledge, very sensibly; so that I proved by my own experience the truth of the following Scriptures (Romans, v. and viii.).

I then (poor mutable worm!) began again
to think, that it was by no means presumptuous
in me to believe that the illuminations which
had been made the instrument of converting
me, and which I had experienced ever since
that time, were divine gifts; for that HE, who
had given His only begotten Son *for me*
amongst other sinners, might also confer these
lesser favours on me.

I also perceived, that these things, though
beautiful and true, were only *means* and not
the end, but merely shadows of that end. I
therefore resolved (a ridiculous word in my
lips) no more to doubt their general truth, and
divine derivation to me; yet, not rashly to
venture to write any thing which I had not
properly digested (which, I began to perceive, had been in great measure the cause of
my failure); but to wait with patience and
resignation, until the course of time, and the
grace of God, should vouchsafe to unravel the
intricate skein of my proper conduct.

[*Five pages of the MS. are here omitted;
being the relation of a dream.*]

From combining and reflecting upon all the
events that had happened to me, I became
again fully persuaded that it was not only
lawful, but in fact my duty, to receive with
gratitude, and apply to the purposes of religious
and moral edification, both to myself and to

the world, the spiritual or figurative sense which I still found to be in myself, and to be continually poured into my mind involuntarily; and which, like an interpreter, explained to me the parables of Scripture and nature. This, therefore, I resolved once for all to do, in spite of the opposition (as I supposed) of my spiritual enemy. Yet as my deficiency in human knowledge, and experimental philosophy, disabled me in great measure from doing justice to these truths, of which, only *the seeds*, as it were, had been given me for cultivation; or, to use a more lively figure, only the unhatched eggs, had been given me for mental incubation; and as I saw, that to propose any thing to the world, in its present enlightened state, in matters of natural philosophy, which would not stand the test of a rigid scrutiny, would only weaken instead of supporting the truth; so I concluded, that the most reasonable and humble thing that I could do, would be to treasure up every thing that I learnt in my mind; to continue to study the Holy Scriptures, with prayer for faith and grace, and, finally, to compare and try every spirit, by this unerring guide and standard of truth, according to the directions of St. John.

With respect to the history of my own conversion, I determined to resume it when I should arrive in Bengal (to which the detach-

ment was then on its return from the Carnatic)
and become more stationary; yet I resolved
not to plunge into those metaphysical depths
which had almost swallowed me up in my late
attempt, but as much as possible to keep in
shallow waters, and not attempt to sail, much
less to walk, upon this great deep. Above all,
I resolved, that in the mean time, since I had
again mingled in some degree in society, my
conduct therein should be such as became the
Gospel of Christ.

In meeting the mess of the corps, I was
often attacked on the subject of religion. On
these occasions, I did not fail to argue boldly
in favour of the Christian faith, and to illustrate my arguments by the help of those parables of nature, which were so luminous, so
convincing to me. But these were either not
understood, or considered as mere accidental
resemblances which proved nothing, but only
tended sometimes to illustrate what was obscure; or lastly, as the mere evaporations of an
imagination overheated and subtilized by the
fire of enthusiasm. When I supported myself
by texts from Holy Scripture, all rational argument was supposed to be at an end; and I was
plainly told, that ignorance and folly were the
groundwork of religious faith; and that such
tales were below the notice of a man of sense,
and of the world.

Hence I continually perceived more clearly, that unless I could reduce my speculations to a regular system, commencing in shadows, or natural things of the most simple and obvious interpretation; and drawing the mind on by degrees to spiritual and intellectual things, in an almost imperceptible manner; and unless this system was founded, like geometry, upon self-evident truths of an universal nature and application; embracing every object of visible creation, and reducing them all as it were to one common denomination, to one general language of divine truth, I should do nothing. Single illustrations, however just and exact, were considered as only casual coincidencies of the infinite forms of imagination and matter, and lost nearly all their force from the want of connexion, on each side, with the adjacent links of the great chain.

From this experience I was convinced, that to address such a mode of argument to the ignorant, gross, and sensual, was like firing shot or cannon balls into an immense mound of mud. They were lost in it, and made no breach, but were not even felt, because the matter was too soft to show the force of the battery by resistance; whereas, the stone walls of deistical philosophy would, I conceived, be easily breached by their own resistance, when opposed by the fire of my analogical artillery,

supported and reinforced by the sword of the
Spirit, which is the word of God. I saw,
therefore, (through the medium of an inex-
perienced and too sanguine imagination) that I
must, if it should please God, address my
speculations to the world at large; and I vainly
trusted, that when the truth of my principles
should be admitted by Christian philosophers*,
the rest of the world would readily receive
them.

Here, many of my Christian readers, who
have not, like me, been lost in the howling
wilderness of infidelity; or, who have not been
brought back to the king's high-way, by the
same unfrequented path, may perhaps say,
this man is quite besotted by his analogies and
parables! He not merely endeavours humbly
to minister to the word of God, and to illustrate its parables by analogy; but he seems to
wish to advance a kind of natural philosophy
from the rank of a servant, to that of an equal,
or associate; and sometimes even to make it
the predominant object in his system. This
will never do. " *Our faith must stand, not in*
" *the wisdom of man, but in the power of God.*"
—1 Cor. ii.

---

* I did not then know that the prejudices of Christian
philosophers were as numerous, and perhaps as strong, as
those of infidels, though of a different kind.

I fully subscribe to the truth of the above sentiments in a general point of view, and only object to them so far as they would impute to me intentions, or at least a bias, which I trust I do not possess. If I know any thing of my own views, respecting analogy, parable, and physico-theological philosophy, they are simply these; viz. I would recommend them to inquirers, just so far as I myself have found them useful; that is to say, subordinately, as admirable illustrators of divine truth; as most lively, delightful, interesting teachers and expositors; as imparting a living spirit to the dead forms of nature, and the dead truths of philosophy; as servants or handmaidens to the word of God.

Having formerly lost my way in the wilderness of error, it pleased the good providence of God to bring me back to His high-way, through this beautiful and flowery path. Can I then do otherwise than recommend it to all who are looking for the right road? Am I wrong to declare to those who may be lost, as I once was, that this path will bring them to the very objects which they are in search of, viz. truth, goodness, happiness? They have only to walk humbly and faithfully in it; and not to consider it as the end, but as a means; not as the mansion to which they look as their final rest, but only as a pleasant road to it, which

shows them that mansion at every turn and
every step.

It might be supposed, that after what I have
already related, respecting my superstitious attention to literal meats, and drinks, and smoking tobacco; as well as the dissipation of my
fears of figurative meats, or doctrines concerning an universal analogy; that what I had
suffered from my folly and want of faith would
have been quite sufficient to preserve me from
similar doubts and scruples in future: yet such
was my weakness, and so numerous were the
artifices of my enemy, that I again fell, and
repeatedly, into the same or similar snares; but
providentially, I was preserved from the terrors
of a broken vow that I once groaned under, in
resuming the practice of smoking, which I had
relinquished as thinking it would be an acceptable sacrifice. After some lapse of time, and
acquisition of knowledge by experience, I al-
tered my opinion, and became persuaded that
my scruples were vain; in consequence of this
change of opinion, I again began to smoke.
Here my conscience, and perhaps my enemy,
accused me of impiety and sacrilege; and it
was long, very long, before I could obtain any
peace of mind. Even years elapsed before I
could be delivered from the overwhelming fear
that I was under the curse of God; not always, but from time to time, as the never-

dying worm took occasion to gnaw the sensibility of my conscience.

These attacks upon the tenderness, or scrupulosity of my conscience, for I am not able to determine what it should be called, resembled the irritating stings and buzzings of musquitos and flies, and sometimes of scorpions; which I by experience discovered to be in some measure natural to my moral and intellectual temperament; for it bred these plagues as naturally as a hot and moist climate does flies, scorpions, and serpents.

In fact, (analogical fact, I mean) heat of climate is emblematic of heat of passion; and much moisture is emblematic of an abundant flow of imagination; and these causes act similarly in the moral and natural cases. A more rational temper is similar to a colder climate, which kills all these tormenting vermin; or rather does not permit them to exist. And the human frigid zone is that of selfish insensibility and philosophical infidelity. Thus both extremes are near death, but by opposite routes.

In reading the New Testament, I particularly attached myself to *our Lord's Sermon on the Mount, which I considered as the measure which I was to fulfil, in order to obtain the promises of the Gospel.* In meditating upon it, I was astonished and staggered at the following Scripture, viz. *" But I say unto you, that ye*

" *resist not evil; but whosoever shall smite thee*
" *on the right cheek, turn to him the other also*,"
&c. &c. I immediately applied this text to the
vexatious, careless, and dishonest conduct of
my native servants; for though I had, since
my supposed conversion, left off chastising
them for their faults, and even speaking roughly
to them ; yet this was by no means a strict and
full obedience to the command; which seemed
rather to require me to encourage them always
to act still worse and worse, and to repeat and
aggravate every offence. Nevertheless, my mind
and heart both revolted in secret against this
intolerable severity, as it often seemed to me to
be, in spite of all my endeavours to smother my
thoughts.

   · But on the other hand, our Lord says in
another chapter of St. Matthew, " *Therefore*
" *all things whatsoever ye would that men should*
" *do to you, do ye even so to them : for this is*
" *the Law and the Prophets.*" This then was
to direct every man to weigh his duty and
regulate his conduct in the balance of reason
and conscience. How to reconcile this law of
true liberty and right reason, with the stern and
seemingly unjust injunction laid down in the
former Scripture, I could not conceive. To
obey both, appeared to me to be impracticable.
Yet as an opening of option was evidently given
by these two distinct, and to my mind opposite

rules; and as one of them appeared to be in
some degree practicable to the weakness of
fallen humanity, assisted by divine grace; and
the other absolutely impracticable without
death, among sinful men, though doubtless perfectly holy and right in itself; so I thought I
might venture to choose that which seemed
most practicable and intelligible to my corrupt
nature.

But in course of time and reading the Gos-
pels, I afterwards observed, that in Mark, ix.
our Lord directs His disciples " *to have salt in*
" *themselves*," and that " *every sacrifice must be*
" *salted with salt*." I understood that salt
was an emblem of *understanding* and *discernment;* and therefore, that this precept implied,
that our obedience and our whole conduct must
be seasoned with *understanding* and *discrimination* in order to be acceptable; and that no
sacrifice could be pleasing to God, which was
not thus salted; for Solomon also says in his
Proverbs, that " *the sacrifice of fools is an*
" *abomination*." Now, allowing this interpretation to be just, which I believed it to be, not
only from the analogy of the thing, but also
from the common observations of men on the
same subject; such as *attic salt*, or wit, and
the custom of the orientals, who say of a foolish
looking man, that there is no *salt* in his face;
also, from the common expression, that hard

sayings must be understood " cum grano
salis *." From all this evidence I concluded,
that all texts of Scripture were not to be taken
and obeyed altogether *literally*, but seasoned
with *salt* of *understanding*. That is to say, *the*
spirit was to be adopted, and *not the letter;*
for as St. Paul says, 2 Cor. iii. " *The letter*
" *killeth, but the Spirit giveth life. Now the*
" *Lord is that Spirit; and where the Spirit of*
" *the Lord is, there is liberty.*" Also our Lord
says in the sixth chapter of St. John, " *It is*
" *the Spirit that quickeneth, the flesh profiteth*
" *nothing.*" And again, " *Judge not according*
" *to the appearance, but judge righteous judg-*
" *ment.*"

In proportion, therefore, as I studied the
Scriptures with a more liberal confidence in the
goodness and mercy of God; or in other
words, in the spirit of adoption, and not in
the letter of the law of bondage; I found my
slavish, legal, superstitious fears and repulsions to yield by degrees to the clear evidence
of the truth. I found, in short, that, as St.
Paul informed me, *I was called unto liberty;*

---

* That is to say, a proper degree of discernment, to
taste, as it were, the hidden sense; and not (as I have heard
some persons say) with a sufficient degree of allowance for
the loose, indefinite, and figurative style of Scripture
parables.

only that I was not to turn this liberty into a cloak of maliciousness, or of sensuality.

Though all these details of my errors, and various absurdities, with many more which I have suppressed, are trifling and tedious in themselves, yet I trust that my Christian readers will see that they were to me instructive lessons, absolutely necessary to correct my strongly legal and self-righteous tendency. But though I was thus harassed incessantly, and, like a person supposed to be bewitched, stumbled at every straw ; yet exclusive of the instruction which I gradually acquired by my experience, I was not without wonderful and divine consolations.

In the first place, *I firmly believed,* that *all would end well.* Secondly, I was amazingly comforted by the precious promises held out in the Scriptures to those who, by perseverance in well doing, seek for eternal life. Thirdly, I was daily delighted, ravished, transported, with the views of infinite wisdom, goodness, beauty, and power, which I enjoyed at the fountain of light and life, the word of God, and in the shadows of them, His works of Creation. These so confirmed each other's testimony, that I could not persist to disbelieve their universal analogy, without being a prodigy of incredulity in myself.

There was no part of Scripture more delightful to me than the Psalms of David; for

they described my own situation, the dangers I
had gone through, and the deliverances which
I had experienced, as exactly as if they had
been composed expressly to describe my own
case. Thus in the 118th Psalm, he says, " *The*
" *Lord is my strength and my song, and is be-*
" *come my salvation! I shall not die, but live,*
" *and declare the works of the Lord. The same*
" *stone which the builders refused is become the*
" *head stone of the corner. This is the Lord's*
" *doing, and it is marvellous in our eyes.*"

Before my poor conversion to Christianity,
and even so far back as when I was a boy in
England, I had a great dislike to the Psalms in
general; partly on account of the writer, whom
I considered as an impious, cruel, hypocritical,
tyrant; and partly because I did not understand what connexion David, or the Jews, or
their affairs, had with the people of Great Bri-
tain. Neither did I at all approve of David's
bitter curses, and harsh treatment of his enemies, which I considered as strange exercises of
religion, and very opposite to the morality of
Christianity ; and therefore I concluded, that
he was not inspired by any thing, except cruelty,
ambition, revenge, and hypocrisy. But now,
the eyes of my understanding being opened
and enlightened by the amplitude of my own
experience, and by the grace of the Holy Spirit, I clearly perceived, and practically felt, that

3

those enemies of David whom he so curses,
were the very same, which had so bitterly per-
secuted me all my life; that is to say, *the
flesh* and *the devil;* and that all the Psalms
were figurative, spiritual, and inspired com-
positions*.

I perceived that the true Israel of God
(Gal. vi.) were the seed of *Abraham, Isaac,*
and *Jacob,* or of *faith, hope,* and *charity,* or
love, through Jesus Christ, in every man's
heart who has them by grace. For who is
Abraham, but the father of the faithful? And
who is *Isaac,* but the seed of promise, or in
other words hope? And who is *Jacob,* that
springs from them, but love, the fruit of faith
and hope? Examine their characters, and they
will be found answerable to the analogy of their
names, or titles. I also perceived, that *the
heathen,* who knew not God, were really, or
spiritually, the evil carnal passions of the unregenerate heart and mind, which are " *the
" children of the wicked one; the enemy that*

---

* That is to say, figurative and spiritual *always,* and
intended literal *sometimes.* " *Doth God take care for oxen?*"
The most literal expressions have always a figurative meaning. Thus every painted portrait has or had a living
original. Thus all prophecies being *spiritual* in their *ultimate scope,* must be spiritually fulfilled; but not being all
literal or *carnal* in their *ultimate scope,* it seems not necessary that they should all be literally fulfilled.

N

" *sowed them is the devil,*" (Matt. xiii. 38, 39.) I
therefore now joined very heartily with the
Psalmist in cursing my enemies, and praying to
God to destroy and root them out of the soil
of my heart.

Hence I saw and felt that every man was a
little world in himself, containing all nations
spiritually in himself. I saw and felt that the
history of the children of Israel, from first
to last, was typical of what had been spiritually
performed, and was still performing, in myself
and all believers, who in like manner were
brought out of Egypt, or the bondage of the
elements of this world, by almighty power!

From this coincidence, which I now concluded
must be general and total *, between natural and
spiritual things, it was again clearly confirmed to
me, agreeably to the above evidence, that the
whole external world, or natural creation in
our planet, was nothing more or less than a
great image of man; and that all the things of
it, of what kind soever, were only shadows of
what was contained in the soul and body of
man†. That the Deity in His infinite wisdom

---

* If any one asks, why I concluded that it must be general and total? I answer, for the same reason that I conclude, that all the propositions of Euclid's twelve books (I
have seen no more) must be true if you admit that the first
is so. The proportions of truth are universal and infinite.

† Thus Solomon says, Ecclesiastes, iii. 11. " Also *He*

had so ordained the course of external nature, as to be perfectly descriptive of, and parallel to, the course of human life both natural and spiritual.

By this means the whole world, both visible and invisible, (including the soul and body of man) was neither more nor less than a grand magazine of testimony to the divine truths of the Bible, divided into two distinct parts; whereof one was body, or shadow, or image, and the other was the spirit, the living substance; and that the whole course of these parallels together, with equal pace, had ever been, was now, and ever must be to the end, a continual demonstration of the truths of the law and the Gospel, by literal matter of fact, as well as by *the analogy* of their forms.

Thus the light of the word of God, and particularly of the New Testament, became to me as the sun of my soul; and human nature became as the earth, which it enlivens and enlightens. Whatever shadow or image I examined in the latter, reflected a light which plainly proceeded from the former; and I often found by experience, (and therefore supposed that it was always the case,) that every com-

---

"*hath set* THE WORLD IN THEIR HEART, *so that no man* " *can find out the work that God maketh, from the beginning* " *to the end."*

pact and condensed light of divine truth, delivered in Holy Scripture, was to be found,
evolved, and displayed in various points of
view, in the eloquent shadows of nature, particularly human nature! so that I was continually exclaiming with the enraptured Psalmist,
" *O Lord my God, Thou art become* EXCEEDING
" GLORIOUS ! *Thou art clothed with* MAJESTY AND
" HONOUR ! *Thou deckest Thyself with* LIGHT
" *as it were with a* GARMENT, *and spreadest out*
" *the* HEAVENS *like a* CURTAIN."—104th Psalm.

Solitude was then no longer dangerous or
frightful to me; for the severe tribulations of
spirit which I had passed through, in the
strength of my Redeemer, had given me such
spiritual patience, experience, and hope, that I
was not afraid nor ashamed; because " the
" love of God was shed abroad in my heart by
" the Holy Ghost."—Romans. Thus all my
trials and persecutions in spirit, which were so
grievous at the time of suffering, were made to
work together for my good. Every snare was
broken, every delusion was gradually dissipated,
and every assault, however severe, was baffled.

When our detachment, on its return to
Bengal, arrived at the famous, or rather in-
famous, Pagoda of Jagrenaut, I surveyed this
temple of Satan, in which the deluded natives
worshipped him under various forms, emblematic of his attributes of death and perdition,

such as toads, serpents, and alligators *, with a
mixture of horror and detestation, which I did
not feel before! For I now interpreted all these
things more spiritually and scripturally; and I
regarded the tyrannical impostors, the Bramins
who keep the temple, as the priests of Satan.

This temple and its environs have been so
fully described by Doctor Buchanan and others,
that there seems to be no necessity for any
further remarks on *them*, which would be little
more than repetitions; but with respect to myself I may observe, that when I considered,
that by nature, and by my former practice, I
was as bad as they; that I was in fact a wor-
shipper of Satan in thought, word, and deed,
and had even been worse than they, as having
sinned against more light; when I considered
all this, I was filled with astonishment and
terror, as well as with joy and gratitude, to
think that I had been permitted, that I had
been *made* to escape! This was certainly a
miracle of grace, for it was quite contrary to
the common course of corrupt nature in man.
I therefore resolved (the same grace preventing
and assisting me) to devote my whole leisure
and capabilities, to the useful purpose of proving and displaying the infinite mercy and glory of

* Not to mention human figures of the most scandalous
description, παρὰ φύσιν.

God in the Christian dispensation; as well as in detecting and developing the snares of the kingdom and powers of darkness! This resolution was sincere and well intended; but I now see, that it was full of ignorance, with not a little presumption, and perhaps some little faith with love.

At that time I had not read any chemical works; yet I perceived from what I did in some small degree comprehend, or as it were smell, without actually seeing, of the nature of chemistry; that, like algebra, it was one of the universal languages of nature, in which she utters, in a mystery, the hidden wisdom of God; describing the progress and warfare of good and evil, life and death, in the human soul and body, as well as in nature in general. I therefore resolved (if it should please God to permit me,) to examine the testimony of this science, to which I thought I found very strong and pointed allusions in the Psalms and Prophets, as well as in the parables of our Lord, and in the writings of St. Paul.

In the same writings I also met with texts, which, by means of the ear of my heart or spirit, gave me a great insight into the realities of which music is a shadow. I felt by this internal ear, which had been opened by the melody and harmony of the word of God, and by the grace of His Holy Spirit, that all

2

the corresponding truths of nature and revelation were true musical harmonies, or symphonious vibrations, and that they were universally established throughout the whole creation; all bearing wonderful, admirable, beautiful witness to the great truths of the glorious
Gospel of Christ.

I felt, or thought I felt, with all the energy
of the self-evidence of the truth in my heart,
which corresponds to the female or sentimental
part of music, or what we call a good ear,
that all the natural sciences were different systems of harmony, subordinate to the divine
subject or theme of Holy Scripture. That a
full and perfect musical composition was a
little type and symbol of the universe; and
that the principal part, the glorious subject to
which all the rest were under-parts, and mere
accompaniments, was the redemption of the
lost world; the victory over death and hell,
sin and Satan; and all the manifestation of the
glory of God in the person and mighty works
of Jesus Christ.

I likewise saw, or thought I saw, that the
male or rational part of music, that is to say,
its mathematical truth of demonstration, tended
equally by *knowledge or sight*, as the female or
sentimental part, by *hearing, or faith*, to prove
the same universal truths; and whatever I saw
in one science, or system, I saw more or less

in every other, according to the attention and faith with which I examined the subject.

But properly to digest and arrange, clearly to detail and illustrate, these infinitudes of spiritual truths to the world; and to give to incorporeal imagery a material substance, a visible and intelligible form; was, I well perceived, an undertaking more than herculean, supposing it in the first place to be lawful. How far this might be the case, I could not yet venture to determine; yet as the various harmonies of my sentiments and thoughts tended continually more and more (as I thought) to form one grand and complete system of spiritual music, the subject of which was the glory of God in our Lord Jesus Christ; so, I was persuaded that I should, some time or other, know it to be lawful and proper to endeavour to display all these witnesses of His infinite majesty to the world*. In the mean time, I was conscious

---

* St. John appears to have had a somewhat similar view of this universe, in the fifth chapter of Revelations, viz. " *And* EVERY CREATURE *which is* IN HEAVEN, *and on* THE " EARTH, *and* UNDER THE EARTH, *and such as are in* THE " SEA, *and all that are* IN THEM, HEARD I, SAYING, BLESS-" ING, *and* HONOUR, *and* GLORY, *and* POWER, *be unto* HIM "·THAT SITTETH UPON THE THRONE, AND UNTO THE LAMB, " *for ever and ever.*" I also heard, with the ears of my mind and heart, a similar chorus arise from all creatures; and as the Apostle's chorus was universal, it must have in-

that nothing could tend more to render the attempt lawful to me, (if it were lawful at all) than by his gracious help to prepare myself for it; first, by a steady course of Christian faith and practice; and secondly, by a humble and diligent study of Holy Scripture, nature, and natural science.

When the march of the Carnatic detachment from Madras back to Bengal was concluded, and we arrived in Calcutta, I remained there only long enough to provide myself with necessaries, and avoided as much as possible to mix with the vain society of the place; but, as may well be supposed, I embraced with unfeigned joy the opportunity thus afforded me of joining in the public worship of my God and Saviour. When I entered the church, to me indeed the temple of the living God, and compared my actual blessed state, with that in which I had quitted Calcutta, to join the Carnatic detachment, my emotions of joy, faith, gratitude, and humble love to our Lord and Saviour were indescribable! But when the organ broke on my ear, which I had not particularly expected, neither was thinking of, the solemn and heavenly tones of the instrument were so perfectly in unison with the

cluded every thing that I heard, and infinitely more than I am able to think or utter, even with the help of analogy.

sentiments then awakened in the harp of my
heart, that I was quite overpowered; and in
spite of all my efforts to restrain myself before
so many spectators, I burst into a flood of joyful rapturous tears.

This sudden and powerful emotion was
fully illustrative of the nature and operations of
music, as connected with the spiritual harmonies
of divine truth in love. Musical instruments
are nothing more or less than images of the
human heart, which the strong threefold combined energy of reason, imagination, and sentiment, under the divine teaching, has invented.
My heart, in itself a musical instrument, was
in perfect unison with the organ, whose tones
were shadows of sentiments of piety and de-
votion; or, divine vital airs of grace and love;
and, therefore, when the fundamental tone of
grateful love (then the master passion) was
thus powerfully agitated by its half spiritual
shadow in natural music, the sympathetic,
symphonious vibrations were full and perfect;
and my inmost soul, being thus forcibly shaken,
communicated its vibrations to my body, which
being also in tune trembled in like manner with
joyful harmony.

I made a point of receiving the Holy Sacra-
ment of the Lord's Supper, which was to me
" meat indeed, and drink indeed," (John). In
performing these duties, I felt an inexpressible

pleasure, because I did them from my heart.
The peace of God which passeth understanding
was there, as well as gratitude, which, blended
with the sense of my own unworthiness and
weakness, penetrated my heart in an indescribable manner.

I embraced the opportunity afforded me by
being in Calcutta, of purchasing some medical
and chemical books, which would, as I trusted,
by divine blessing, give me much assistance.
Yet, even at this more advanced period, I was
still so much afraid of being impious and presumptuous, that I debated the matter within
myself repeatedly, before I was able to decide
on the lawfulness of using such a means to
promote my good designs; that is to say, of
using the labours of *probable infidels*, to increase and establish true faith. But at last, I
was persuaded and satisfied that they contained
" *the heritage of the heathen* *," which the
Lord in His good pleasure had given to me, as
he had formerly given the Kingdoms of Canaan
to His own people; and that it was my duty to
take them in possession, and use them to His
honour and glory, through Jesus Christ. Thus

---

* That is to say, true, natural, and experimental philosophy and science, which, figuratively, is the outer court
of the temple of religion, which is given to the Gentiles,
who often, too often, trample prophanely on the temple.

the Psalmist says, Psalm cxi. " *He hath showed* " *His people* THE POWER OF HIS WORKS, *that He* " *may give them the* HERITAGE OF THE HEATHEN." Thus, the natural works of God have been *pro- verbially,* as it were, given to the heathen, or to in- fidel natural philosophers, who have abused them, as mentioned by St. Paul in the first chapter to the Romans; and as in our own days the self- called philosophers of the revolutionary school have done. But when it pleases God to open the understanding of any believer, to see the secret analogy existing between His word and His works, then " *He shows them* THE POWER " OF HIS WORKS, *that He may give them* THE " HERITAGE OF THE HEATHEN." It was given kindly to the heathen, to lead them on, if pos- sible, to the *secret spirit,* which is the proper heritage of His own people. As our Lord says, " *To you it is given to know the mysteries of the* " *kingdom of heaven; but to them it is not given.* " *Therefore speak I to them in parables."* This is like the outer court given to the Gentiles.— See Revelations, xi.

I soon perceived, that the ignorance of in- fidel writers, concerning the true spirit and meaning of the testimonies which they recorded, was a pledge in general of their veracity; for had they suspected that they were thus under- mining their own foundations, and pulling down their own house, not a word would they

3

have truly published. But the power and wisdom of God were displayed more gloriously in thus making his enemies bear witness for Him, in those things which they intended against HIM. Thus, " *He taketh the wise in their* " *own craftiness.*"—1 Cor.

Perhaps, nothing tended more to assist me in my progress, and to obviate all the difficulties which impeded my advance, than the gradual application of a discovery which had been made to me at a very early period of my researches; viz. that all things *in nature* were *algebraic*, or *double*, as well as in the moral and spiritual worlds; that is, both plus and minus, good and evil, although there was only one common set of symbols, to express both of these opposite scales, For instance, to begin with a very simple case, a vertical straight line produced from the earth towards heaven, typifies in Scripture language, as well as in its own natural conditions, a perfect religious tendency in a man, who is therefore called an *upright* man; but if the tendency of the same line be inverted, or supposed to tend from heaven towards the centre of the earth, then it will denote an apostacy, or a falling from spiritual to carnal things.

Again, the action of leaven, *which is an intestine war, between two opposite principles,* is by our Lord compared to the progress of the

kingdom of God in the human heart; but the
very same operation is, by St. Paul, compared
to the progress of the kingdom of Satan in the
heart of man; that is to say, " *the leaven of*
" *malice and wickedness*."—1 Cor. v.

Again, the Holy Spirit descended upon the
Apostles under the emblem of " *cloven tongues*,
" *like as of fire*." But a cloven or double
tongue is the mark of the dragon, and of the
beast of the earth, in the Book of Revelations,
and it is an emblem of *equivocation**. Also,
St. Paul exhorts Timothy " *to show himself*
" *approved to God, a workman that needeth not*
" *to be ashamed*, RIGHTLY DIVIDING THE WORD OF
" TRUTH."—Chap. ii. Lastly, the brazen serpent is considered as an emblem of our Lord
Jesus Christ; hence, those who contend *that
the parables of Holy Scripture are not to be
taken strictly, and that they seldom hold if we
descend to minute particulars*, have no right to
make this objection, until they have entirely
examined both sides of the question; that is
to say, both the *positive* and *the negative characteristics*. If they do this completely, they
will find a degree of accuracy in the most
minute particulars, that will astonish them!

* " And he had two horns like a lamb, *and he spake as*
" *a dragon*."—Chap. xiii.

Without this *clue* and *master key*, I could never have got on.

The application of all these *shadows*, to their proper respective *substances* of good and evil, in the human soul, was generally very obvious to me; and even when it was not so, at the time when I most studied the subject, yet it very frequently occurred to me clearly, when I least expected it, and even when I thought upon matters wholly unconnected therewith in appearance. This was a natural consequence of the truths and principles above stated. All parts of nature seem to be intimately connected, as it were, by a common sensorium, and communication of nervous fluid of truth, if I may so speak, which pervades the whole; but our sight is too feeble and short to discover these connexions, except by experience, in the course of those events which we term *accident*; but which are parts of the secret, regular, and lively mathematical plan of the great Governor of the universe.

I perceived, by help of the above experience, that to enable the rays of *spiritual light*, or *divine truth*, to enter my mind and pass freely, to illuminate my internal darkness effectually, and become visible to others, it was necessary that my soul should become spiritually *transparent*, like glass, or crystal; and I saw that this could only be done by *the purification of my heart*, whose corruptions and doubtings rendered the eye of my understanding dark, and impervious to the truth. Thus St. James says, " PURIFY *your* HEARTS, *ye* DOUBLE MINDED," or, *purge and fast, ye dim sighted, or double sighted.*

Here the mysteries of light and shade were (as I thought) in some degree opened to my view. I saw that the rays of light from the sun resembled perfectly the rays of truth from the word of God; and that though they were on all sides equally dispensed by His infinite goodness, yet that an impure, sensual, and unbelieving heart, was equally unable to display or distinguish, or reflect them, as a lump of dirt, or a common stone. But I understood that this dirt, or stone, might be so refined and purified in *the furnace of trial and affliction,* through the operation of *the vital air, of the spirit of life and truth,* as to become transparent or enlightened throughout, like glass, and therefore freely to admit, reflect, transmit, and be illuminated by the colours of heaven *. These I understood to be the Christian virtues, or graces of faith, hope, and love; with all their modifications, proceeding from our Lord and Saviour; and from His holy word of truth.

* My reader will perceive that I allude here to the manufacture of glass, which is made by burning sand and alkali.

This conception was confirmed by the following passage in the Revelations: " *And he* " *carried me away in the spirit to a great and* " *high mountain*" (or a spiritual elevation), " *and* " *showed me that great city, the holy Jerusalem,* " *descending out of heaven from God, having* " *the glory of God: and her light was like unto* " *a stone most precious, even like a jasper* " *stone, clear as crystal. And the building* " *of the wall of it was jasper; and the city* " *was pure gold, like unto clear glass. And* " *the foundations of the wall of the city were* " *garnished with all manner of precious stones.*" Chap. xxi.

But the new and heavenly Jerusalem is a figurative and spiritual city, or in plain terms the church triumphant, *the bride of Christ;* therefore in Scripture language all churches are described as *women,* or *cities* having *husbands;* and even the oriental heathens use these figures. They call kings by the title of *Shaheriar,* or *the layer of the city.* Now the foundations of this city are, *faith, hope, charity;* and all the Christian graces; which proceed from *Christ, the corner stone, elect and precious* of this city; in whom they concentre, and are self-existent. *The gold* of this city *is faith*;* and though,

* Therefore yellow typifies faith, blue hope, and red love. This will be proved hereafter, if it pleases God. Blood is red, and it is life, and life is love, or love is life.

o

in this present state, our faith is *obscure* or *opaque*, or without clear light of knowledge, yet in the church triumphant, and in our heavenly state, it will be full of the light of perfect knowledge, or *transparent*. For now we see through " a glass darkly, (a smoked " glass) but then face to face; now I know in " part: but then shall I know, even as also I " am known."—1 Cor. xiii. Also St. Paul says to the Romans, " For *hope* that is *seen*, is *not* "*hope*; for that which a man *seeth*, why doth "* he yet *hope for* ?—Chap. viii.

The above description of the Holy Jerusalem, given by St. John, demonstrated also the spiritual and typical nature of geometry (which is the law of God in visible nature) as fully to my understanding, as it did that of light. He says, " *And the city lieth* FOUR-" SQUARE, *and the* LENGTH *is as large as the* " BREADTH; *and he measured the city with the* " REED * *twelve thousand furlongs. The* LENGTH, " *and the* BREADTH, *and the* HEIGHT *of it are* " EQUAL." That is to say, *the holy city, the church triumphant, the bride of Christ*, is truly represented by the form of the *cube*. Therefore, that form must have a spiritual resemblance to the perfect holiness and righteousness of the elect in Christ.

* The *golden reed of the analogy of faith*, as I suppose.

Happily, the spirit of the cube and square
is not difficult of extraction, by means of the
help of their analogies. When a man acts
honestly and *uprightly*, we denominate his conduct to be *fair* and *square*. Now we cannot
deny this to be a very strong testimony, without contradicting the common sense of mankind. But the matter is susceptible of a demonstration as strong and perfect, though of a
mixed nature, as any proposition in Euclid, if
we admit the existence of moral and spiritual
demonstration.

A straight line, or path, is a figurative expression among men, denoting true moral conduct; and a crooked line, or path, is equally
figurative of false or erroneous moral conduct.
If this testimony stood alone upon its own
foundation, it might be called a vulgar notion,
destitute of authority; but this is not the case,
the similitude is borrowed from the word of
God. Thus the Prophet Isaiah says, " *The*
" WAY *of peace they know not* ; *and there is*
" *no judgment in their* GOINGS: *they have made*
" *them* CROOKED PATHS : *whosoever* GOETH *therein*
" *shall not know peace.*"—Chap. lix. 8.

Again, chap. xl. " *The voice of him that*
" *crieth in the wilderness, Prepare ye the way*
" *of the Lord, make* STRAIGHT *in the desert a*
" HIGHWAY *for our God.*" Now all Christian
believers allow the above expressions to be

figurative, or to have a spiritual meaning. They
believe the Gospel to be the *way*, the *high way*
of salvation; and they believe it to be the only
way to fulfil the holy law of perfect truth and
righteousness.

Upon these undisputed foundations, therefore,
I venture to try to develope and demonstrate
the analogies of the cube and square.

A straight line being the true emblem (not
only among men, but in the word of God also)
of truth and moral rectitude, therefore a vertical
straight line, as being such a line directly produced from earth towards heaven, is typical of
the line of true *religious* piety, which has precisely the same direction in a spiritual sense.
Therefore, in Holy Scripture, a faithful and
religious man is called an *upright man*, or to
speak geometrically, a *vertical* man; as the
Lord says of Job, " *A* PERFECT *and an* UPRIGHT
" MAN ; *one that feareth God, and escheweth*
" *evil.*"

Again, if the said vertical straight line be
bisected at right-angles, by another equal
straight line, so that this other straight line be
also bisected by the first; then this second line
is an emblem, equally true and perfect, of the
line or *path* of true moral rectitude. For the
line of true morality is closely connected with
the line of true religion. But how? It is not
parallel, for then they would never meet, nor

enter into each other, as it is plain they do from Scripture; for St. Paul says, "*Whether, " therefore ye eat, or drink, or whatsoever ye do, "* DO ALL TO THE GLORY OF GOD."—1 Cor. x.

Hence it is evident, that every, even the most common action of moral-natural life and conduct, is an act of religion in a subordinate degree and manner. Since then the straight line of religion and the straight line of morality do meet and enter into each other, that is to say, intersect each other, in what manner and degree is this intersection performed?

First, let it be supposed that the angle of intersection is less than a right angle on one side of the vertical line, and consequently greater than a right angle on the other side of the same; also, that neither of the said straight lines bisect each other. Then the second or moral straight line, being divided and regulated by the first, or vertical straight line of religion*, therefore, one part of the moral line, on one side of the vertical, does, and must necessarily typify that part of morality which regards our neighbour; and the other part of the same, on the other side of the vertical, does, and must

---

* The love of God is the great commandment, and the first; the second or love of man "*is like unto it,*" but not equal in degree or in kind, because it is mixed with self-love in equal measures.

symbolize that part of morality which regards ourself: for these two parts, viz. *self-love* and *social-love*, do make up the sum total of the moral line, which is divided by every man's *religion*, or *conscience towards God*. Now because the two straight lines do not bisect each other, but only intersect each other in points distant from their respective centres; therefore, the two distinct parts of the moral line above-mentioned will not be equal; for the intersections of the lines not being in the centre of each, therefore one side shall be more than a true radius, and the other side shall be less than a true radius. Therefore the *practical*, or *linear* * measurement of our duty and love to our neighbour, will not be equal to the measure of our *practical* duty and love to ourselves. Also, the angles on each side of the vertical line being the *speculative* measures, respectively, of our love and duty to our neighbour and ourselves, are also unequal from the construction. But the law of God and of perfect truth says, " *Thou shalt love thy neighbour as thyself.*" Hence it is evident, that oblique angles, and unequal radii, cannot be the true construction

---

* In surveys, we measure distances, or lines, by the chain, *practically;* but we measure angles *speculatively*, by a sight, or glass, and without moving from our place. The last denotes theory, the first experiment.

of the moral line, with respect to the true religious line; and it is equally evident, that no construction of the said moral straight line, except that which is at right angles to, and in mutual bisection of, the religious and moral lines, can be the true moral straight line, as described and constructed by our Lord Jesus Christ, both by precept and in practice.

From what has been said it is evident, that the diagram supposed above, is a true type of the whole law of God, viz. " *Thou shalt love* " *the Lord thy God, with all thy heart, and* " *mind, and soul, and strength; and thou shalt* " *love thy neighbour as thyself*." Now, we have only to join the adjacent extremities, of this rectangular and equilinear CROSS, by straight lines; and we shall have the *square* type of the *New Jerusalem*, which, multiplied by its root, produces the *cube* of the same *.

In the square thus formed, the sides, or external limits of the figure, are emblematic of *practical* and *oblique*, or *moral* conduct, as denoted by the moral ∠ of 45° on each extremity; and the internal and perpendicular lines and angles are figures of *square*, or *conscientious*

---

* The square and cube here demonstrated, are spiritually formed, by the *circumcision* of four segments of *the circle*, and six solid segments of *the sphere* of humanity, by the law of truth in love.

and *speculative* measurement. The radius typifies *the letter* of *the law* in speculation, equal
to the chord of 60° only; whereas the true
exterior or practical measure, required by the
square spirit of the radius, is equal to the chord
of 90°. The true Christian, in his practical conduct, measures, or strives to measure, the latter
to his neighbour ; and the legal hypocrite measures the chord of 60°, which he says is equal
to the radius, or visible tangible letter of the
law. The solution of this ambiguity is in the
consideration, that the internal measure is
square in both radii, and the external is oblique,
and therefore must be lengthened so as to
equal the internal square measure of both the
religious and moral radii. Therefore the chord
of 90°, is no greater nor less in square measure, than the square of the moral radius,
added to the square of the religious radius, both
of which are to be combined in all our actions,
in order to give them the full complement required by the holy law. This has been already
proved, viz. " Whether therefore ye eat or
" drink, or whatsoever ye do, do all to the glory
" of God."—1 Cor. x.

The same figure of the cross presents Christians with another awfully interesting parable,
admirable for its comprehensiveness. This
cross being a type of the whole law of God, to
which it was our duty to be for ever *conformed;*

and we having broken this holy law, and departed from it in all respects, therefore our condign punishment was to be made conformed thereto by just though severe force; for our nature was become so corrupt, so contrary to the law, that to be made to conform strictly to it was to us the most cruel of torments, and well represented in external shadows by the figure of a *man nailed to a wooden cross.*

This punishment then showed us what we as sinners deserved to suffer; not, indeed, properly as punishment, but as the mere discharge of a duty eternally binding, as the just demands of the law only. The punishment for the breach of the law appears to be distinct from, and in addition to this. Yet this alone would doubtless appear sufficient to most men, even as a punishment. But the Lord suffered thus in our stead; and by being thus made conformed to the cross and torment of the law, for us, He delivered us from it and from the penalties of its breach; which penalties he also suffered *for us,* as our surety.

The above may suffice to give a slight intimation of the clear, accurate, universal, and almost infinite analogies of the whole body of mathematics; every proposition of which, from first to last, is a true, exact, and instructive parable, demonstrative of intellectual, moral, and religious truths. But the knowledge of the first principles of good and evil is perhaps all that is necessary to be demonstrated, except in case of controversy.

The grand ultimate use then of science, and philosophy, the merciful and gracious intention of the Creator in placing all these His glorious works before us, as well as *in us*,[*] and in giving us *reason, imagination*, and *sentiment*, His three witnesses on earth [†], to enable us to understand and feel them; is, doubtless, to lead us on by degrees from earth to heaven, from natural things to spiritual things, from human philosophy to the wisdom of God, and the glory of God, as displayed in our Lord Jesus Christ.

If philosophers reason in any other manner than this, they are not truly wise; that is to say, not wise unto salvation. If we suppose that God gave us ability to explore *His works*, all of them *holy* and *righteous;* and to demonstrate His holy law of truth and proportion, in

---

* Also, " He hath set *the world in their heart*, so " that no man can find out the work that God maketh, from " the beginning to the end."—Ecclesiastes, iii. 11.

† They are not only so generally speaking, and in a manner so very obvious that no one can deny or call it, in question; but I also suspect that they are *the very three witnesses*, whom St. John means when he says in his general Epistle, chap. v. " *There are three that bear witness in* " *earth*, THE SPIRIT, *and* THE WATER, *and* THE BLOOD; *and* " *these three agree in one.*"

inanimate nature founded in perfect wisdom, power, and goodness, for the mere purpose of gratifying *our fleshly lusts*, or adorning those *creeping things* with the embellishments of a degraded science, and a carnal or animal philosophy, falsely so called; we then become a kind of idolaters, as St. Paul shews, Romans, i. viz.

"*For the wrath of God is revealed from*
"*heaven against all ungodliness, and unrigh-*
"*teousness of men,* WHO HOLD THE TRUTH IN
" UNRIGHTEOUSNESS : *because that which may*
"*be known of God*" (from His works) "*is*
"*manifest in them; for God hath shewed it unto*
"*them.* FOR THE INVISIBLE THINGS OF HIM,
" FROM THE CREATION OF THE WORLD, ARE CLEARLY
" SEEN, BEING UNDERSTOOD BY THE THINGS THAT
" ARE MADE, *even His eternal power and* GOD-
" HEAD; *so that they are without excuse; because*
"*that,* WHEN THEY KNEW GOD *they glorified*
"*Him* not AS GOD, *neither were thankful;*
"*but became vain in their imaginations, and*
"*their foolish heart was darkened. Professing*
"*themselves to be* WISE, *they became* FOOLS, *and*
"*changed the glory of the uncorruptible God*
"*into* AN IMAGE MADE LIKE TO CORRUPTIBLE MAN;
"*and to* BIRDS, *and* FOUR-FOOTED BEASTS, *and*
" CREEPING THINGS," &c. &c.

I have now laid before my readers the sum and sequel of my wanderings in the great

wilderness of the world, as well as of my poor
conversion, until 1794. What then is the fruit
of my eventful experience?

I have explored many a devious path in
search of happiness, and this is the result of
my inquiries and labours. *Perfect happiness*
is inseparable from *perfect goodness ;* hence it
is only to be found in God, who is the source
of both. But God is in heaven, and we crawl
upon the earth! Such knowledge is too wonderful and excellent for man; he cannot attain
unto it! We cannot find out God by our own
wisdom and goodness, any more than we can
fly to the sun.

Our great Creator, and most merciful Father, knowing this, has most graciously provided
us with a true and faithful guide, in His own
dearly beloved, only begotten Son. " HE IS
" THE WAY, THE TRUTH, and THE LIFE ; *no man*
" *cometh unto the Father, but through* HIM."—
St. John.

To HIM therefore, with the *Father,* and *the
Holy Ghost,* ONE, GOD, Almighty ! be ascribed,
as is most due, all honour, praise, glory, and
dominion, for ever and ever. Amen.

POSTSCRIPT.

———

THE foregoing Narrative, which was begun in
1793, and finished in 1794, both inclusive, concluded as above. At present, taking a re-
vised and extractive copy of it (in the year
1809), it appears to me not impertinent, to add
my actual now existing views of the subject of
a universal analogy, which occupies so great a
part of the work.

*After near sixteen years of experience and
observation, my opinion of the truth, beauty,
and importance of this species of intellectual
sight, this telescopic and microscopic view of
visible and invisible things, is not changed as to
the thing itself*; yet time, and the said experience, have brought to my consideration and
feeling, various weighty obstacles which oppose,
as well as some views which encourage, its cultivation.

Though analogy, or proportion, on the basis
of right reason and revelation, is a powerful
supporter of the faith of Christ, and like Paul
mighty in expounding the Scriptures, yet it

2

requires like Paul the aid of a *Barnabas* to
introduce it to *the church,* who do not believe
that it is a *disciple;* but consider it as a wolf in
sheep's clothing, a heathen philosopher (or,
what is thought as bad, a kind of *Hutchin-
sonian)* in disguise *.

No man will believe or receive analogies of
an evangelical appearance and tendency, who is
not a real Christian, or under a course of train-
ing in the hand of God to become one; *for
when a thing is capable of two interpretations,
a man will never choose that which he dislikes,
and which it has been the practice, if not the
study, of his life to avoid. Now analogy is
always double, or susceptible of two interpretations; or, in other words, it is* ALGEBRAIC, *or a
sword with two edges.* "*It speaks as a dragon.*"
Revelations, xiii. The positive part is "*a savour
of life, unto life,*" and the negative part is "*a
savour of death, unto death.*"—2 Cor. ii. If
the study of the first, or positive part, be highly
profitable to Christians unto edification, the
study of the second, or negative part, is equally

* But I *can,* and *do,* truly assure my readers, that
though I began to study universal analogy in some degree,
before the year 1790; yet I never heard of *Hutchinson,* or
Hutchinsonians, before the year 1814; when the Rev. Mr.
Jones of Nayland's books were put into my hands by the
Rev. Daniel Corrie, as a work which would please me, being
so consonant to opinions which he had heard me express.

3

deadly to infidels, to destruction; for it furnishes arms tempered in Stygian waters, or *that sword of Satan* which nothing can resist, " *but the* " *sword of Michael, from the armoury of God,* " *tempered so, that neither keen nor solid may* " *resist that edge.*"—See Paradise Lost, Book VI.

The enemies of the Gospel seem to have already discovered the reality and power of *universal analogy,* and have used it effectually; for instance, in the French Revolution, and ever since. Their spiritual head has revealed to them the negative part, or rather the negative interpretation which may be put upon that truth, which in its direct and true sense is positively good and vital*; and I am sorry to say, that they appear to be more wise and enlightened in their generation than the children of light. The latter seem to be less afraid of the sword of Satan in the hands of his soldiers, than of the sword of the Gospel in the hands of their own.

But it may be said, in opposition to all that has been here asserted, that even if it be so, Christians do not need this sword; but may safely reject so dangerous a weapon, and so

* Satan has fought in this manner from the beginning, viz. " *Ye shall be as gods, knowing good and evil.*" They did not know that there were *infernal gods.* He kept his word, but he had *a double tongue, like a serpent.*

equivocal an ally. It is no where said in Scripture, that the study or belief of analogy is necessary to salvation. The saints, martyrs, and confessors, have hitherto entered into life without it, *at least without making it a professed study*. What then is its necessity or use, except occasionally, and by way of illustration; in which way all use it, without making so much ado about it? Cannot this man be content with the advantage of drawing privately from this fund, whenever he requires it, without calling aloud upon all men to come and share the hidden treasure which he pretends to have found in his field? The man in the thirteenth chapter of St. Matthew, who finds the Gospel treasure, is said *immediately to hide it*; we suspect, therefore, that these are not the true riches, which this man displays so ostentatiously.

But those who thus think, do not consider that our LORD is not narrating THE LIFE *of a convert*, in the thirteenth chapter of St. Matthew; He is only describing his feelings on first discovering the hidden treasure of the Gospel, and before he has made it his own by purchasing the field. In this early stage he fears to lose the precious deposit, and therefore very wisely hides it until he has procured a true title to it. After that period, it cannot be supposed that he

continues to hide what is so honourable and
beneficial to himself, and to all his neighbours,
who are called to participate with him. The
Parable of the Lost Sheep, and Silver Pieces,
authorises this exposition, and removes the objection so far ; that is to say, if the reader will
permit me to consider the Lost Sheep and Silver
Piece, as the truth of the Gospel which I had
lost.

It is true, that analogy, considered abstractedly, is only an interpreter and guide, and is
not immediately necessary to salvation, generally and loosely speaking. It is like Philip to
the eunuch ; it is like the interpreter's house in
the Pilgrim's Progress; it is like a dictionary to a
person who is learning a language; and though
it may be contended that there is no necessity
to learn it by rote, yet surely the more we
consult it and know of it, the greater progress
we shall make. Faith in our Lord Jesus Christ,
is undoubtedly the bread and meat of eternal life;
or at least the procuring cause of it. " *Whoso*
" *eateth my flesh, and drinketh my blood, hath*
" *eternal life;*" says our Lord to the unbelieving Jews (John, vi.). It is evident that faith
was what the Jews immediately wanted ; faith
to induce them to receive the bread and meat
of life, which the Lord graciously offered to
them. But supposing that they had, through
faith, received and eaten this food of the soul,

still, unless they had also digested it, it would
have passed through them without affording
due nourishment. Now the salt of analogy is
necessary to *digest* the food of the soul, that
is, to *understand* it, particularly when it is
hid under the form of parable. What then is
the object of food? Is it not digestion in the
first place, and strength in the second? Strength
to walk, to act, to perform the duties of life.
Digestion, therefore, is equally necessary with
food, being equally a means towards the same
end; and understanding is equally necessary
with faith; for St. Paul says to the Ephesians,
" *Till we all come in the unity of the* FAITH, *and*
" *of the* KNOWLEDGE *of the Son of God, unto a*
" PERFECT MAN, *unto the* MEASURE *of the* STA-
" TURE *of the* FULNESS *of* CHRIST; *that we*
" *henceforth be no more* CHILDREN."

The disciples heard the parables of the Lord
as well as the other Jews, and they heard them
with faith in their truth and importance, which is
evinced by their desire to have them explained.
But they understood not, and therefore, *in spite
of their faith,* the food which they had received,
would not have strengthened them, had not
our Lord afterwards explained the meaning.
Here then we have an example of the use of
analogy. In attending to His explanations,
they perceived that *natural things are emblems
of spiritual things,* and that by means of the

analogies or *proportions* of the former, we comprehend the latter, which are otherwise inscrutable to fleshly eyes and ears *.

Natural salt is not immediately necessary to life; but it is necessary to digestion, to relish, and to discrimination. Yet who but a savage would reject the use of salt, because he can live uncomfortably and unhealthily without it? or because it will not support life by itself, without bread and meat, which it was intended to season and improve, but not to supersede?

What does St. Paul say upon this subject? I beg my reader to consider it well. He says to the Hebrews, chap. v. "*We have many* " *things to say, and hard to be uttered, seeing ye* " *are dull of hearing. For when for the time ye* " *ought to be teachers, ye have need that one* " *teach you again which be the first principles* " *of the oracles of God; and are become such as* " *have need of* MILK, *and not of* STRONG MEAT. " *For every one that useth* MILK *is unskilful in* " *the word of righteousness: for he is a babe.* " *But* STRONG MEAT *belongeth to them that are of* " FULL AGE, *even those who by reason of use* " *have their senses exercised, to discern both* " *good and evil*" (that is, to digest).

* It may be said, that the Holy Spirit of Truth alone can enable us to understand these parables, even when they are opened. This I allow, and hope that some of my readers may ask for it.

From this Scripture it is evident, that those who oppose the use of analogy in religion, do resolve to be babes in it all their lives, and as far as possible to keep all other Christians in the same childish state. It may be said to them *in point of fact,* though not as to *intention,* "*Ye have taken away* THE KEY OF KNOWLEDGE; "*ye entered not in yourselves, and them that* "*were entering in ye hindered.*"

But many will probably say, that the analogies displayed by me are not real analogies, but mere fanciful reveries of a disordered imagination. They will, perhaps, load them with the charge of folly, presumption, and impiety; and lastly, they will probably declare their opinion, that they would be destructive of religion, by inducing *weak minds* to believe that all religion is a creature of the imagination! I have heard such objections.

But I may, I believe, truly observe, that the Bible itself has had this very consequence; which they deprecate, upon weak minds. For instance, all those multitudes of deists and atheists, with which the world always swarms, would probably, nay I believe certainly, have remained satisfied with any of the various kinds of poly-theism, which formerly covered the almost whole earth. To the absurdities of those superstitions they would have had no objection, but would have remained very re-

ligious men in their way, had not the Gospel
appeared. But the sun of revelation has extinguished all those rushlights ; and, unfortu-
nately for *weak minds*, it is as much too luminous for their feeble sight, as the others are now
too dark; and the consequence is, that they
will have none at all; because too much light
is as bad as too little. They are ashamed now
of the one, and afraid of the other. The analogy of faith, or the analogy of the *word* and
the *works* of God, may have this effect upon
such *weak minds* as are mentioned above; and
the more luminous, abundant, and admirable
it is, the greater will such effect be, as in the
case of the Scriptures themselves.

Those who object to any particular and proposed analogies, on the ground that they are
false, or inapplicable, ought to make themselves
tangible; ought to show that they are false in a
regular and satisfactory manner. If they will
not or cannot do this, they will perhaps do
well to follow the example of Gamaliel. Acts, v.

POSTSCRIPT II.

Written in 1823.

N**early** fourteen years have elapsed, since I wrote the foregoing P. S. in A. D. 1809; and now taking the fourth, and probably the last copy of the same Narrative in 1822-3, at the particular request of Christian friends, I still think it necessary to state my present sentiments respecting a *universal analogy* between the visible and invisible works of God.

Every day's experience confirms me in the conviction, that it (a universal analogy) is a matter of fact, and that it is the work of the God of truth, ordained for the most important purposes; which will appear more clearly, illustriously, and triumphantly, in proportion to the lapse of time.

If any one shall ask, what are these important purposes? I would answer, that I believe they are, not only *generally*, the increase of faith and knowledge, in the study of both physical and metaphysical subjects, which I feel to be true from experience and observation, together with all the rest of the thinking world, more or less; but also, I believe, (which perhaps the rest of the world do not) that the most important of them is, *the manifestation of divine truth, the revelation of Jesus Christ to the soul!* But how? I reply, by opening figurative passages of Scripture, and symbolical prophecies in particular*.

For instance, St. John says, Revelations, chap. i. " *Behold, He (Christ) cometh with* " *clouds.*" The two angels in the first of the Acts, the Prophet Daniel, the Evangelists, and our Lord, say the same. Did the reader never see *the sun* break forth suddenly through openings of *dark clouds,* and dazzle the world with unexpected glory? But, these are only *natural clouds,* they are not the clouds of *that heaven,* in which " *the Son of man*" (spiritually) " *cometh.*" Christ is figuratively *the sun* of our heaven; and *our heaven* is figuratively *the word of God,* more especially *the Gospel of our Lord Jesus Christ* †. What then are the *clouds*

---

* As *a ladder* which reacheth from earth to heaven. Genesis.—And, as a *golden reed.* See note on the analogies of matrimony, both spiritual and natural. Page 110, and following, of the Narrative. Also, Rev. xxi.

† The natural sun, and the natural heavens, are only types of the spiritual anti-types.

of *our heaven?* Let " *the stewards of the*
" MYSTERIES *of God**" answer this question.

David says, Psalm cviii. " *Thy truth reacheth*
" *unto* THE CLOUDS. But the natural clouds of
this earth are a very short range for that truth
which pervadeth all the worlds! To compare
small things with the greatest, as well might an
artillerist tell us that a twenty-four-pounder
cannon, loaded with a full charge of powder,
will throw its ball six feet! All reflecting men
would see the absurdity of such a statement
immediately: I therefore venture to say, as a
paraphrase, that the truth of the word of God
shines gloriously to the eyes of our minds, until
it is obscured or lost to our sight, in the " MYS-
" TERIES *of the kingdom of heaven.*" But our
Lord tells us in the thirteenth chapter of St.
Matthew, that His parables contain " THE MYS-
" TERIES *of the kingdom of heaven!* When
these *dark sayings,* these *clouds* are opened by
analogy, then *the sun of righteousness* appears
in His glory, through the medium of *faith†.*

But our Lord says also, in chap. xviii. of
St. Luke, " *When the Son of man cometh,*
" *shall He find faith on the earth?*"

---

* Fourth of Corinthians.

† See all the parables of our Lord; and all the Proverbs
of Solomon, which are a book of clouds. Also, the Psalms,
Also, 2 Peter, ii. and Jude, verse 12.

Every reader must answer this question for himself. Does he think, that if he suddenly beheld the Lord Christ revealed in glory from behind a natural cloud, together with His mighty angels, in flaming fire*, with the sound of the trump of God, that he could possibly disbelieve the evidence of his senses? If he says, *no, it is impossible that I could disbelieve that*, then he will be constrained by truth to confess, that *the clouds of heaven* above spoken of, and *the coming of the Son of Man in those clouds*, must be spiritual, intellectual, and moral; and not visible, literal, and natural; and consequently, that there will be a coming of the Son of Man, when He will only be seen through the medium of faith.

If this be granted, the next thing required, will be to discover some *spiritual clouds* of the *spiritual heaven*; more likely to be meant by the inspired writers, than those of its *mysteries*.

Under this view of the subject, if any reader denies the reality and importance of an universal analogy, he will very probably be the man who will be found to have no faith when the Son of Man cometh: for, He cometh, first, in the plainest parts of the Gospel; and after-

---

* 2 Thessalonians, i. and 1 Corinthians, xv.

wards in *the clouds,* of *the mysteries*,* or *pa-rables* of the word of God; but when they are truly opened by the analogy of faith, then those who read, or hear, but perceive him not, *in spirit,* have either not faith, or not sight.

That there will be a literal visible advent of the Lord Jesus Christ, the writer, after mature consideration, does not find it difficult to be-lieve; for perhaps nothing less will convince the world at large, full as it is of learning and philosophy, co-operating with impiety, to com-pose an intense *freezing mixture* for the soul; and stirred up by three unclean spirits of devils, viz. superstition, infidelity, and anar-chy †. But He will then appear to sight I presume, and not only to faith; for faith implies the absence of sight. He will then come to judge, to reward and to punish ; but not as an object of faith, I apprehend.

At the same time, the writer does not here

---

* Doubtless, *they* are more blessed and acceptable who believe on the simple evidence of the plainest parts of Scrip-ture ; yet since it has pleased the abounding grace of God to grant the additional testimony of the knowledge of opened mysteries, which speak the same things as the plain parts by analogy, ought we not to receive them with lively gratitude?

† I am ready to give up these three evil spirits, if any other three worse can be found; but these seem to be pre-dominant in the world at present, and afford no mean proof that Mr. Faber may be correct in thinking that we are now under the influence of the sixth vial.

mean to allude to the last judgment, but to the asserted supposed coming of the personal Word of God on the white horse, to destroy the beast and the false prophet, and to establish the millennium *.

The controversy which has lately sprung up, between the advocates of a merely spiritual advent and reign upon earth, of Messiah, during one thousand years, and those of a literal and visible advent and reign, has unawares led the writer into these remarks; or at least, into this application of the subject of an *universal analogy*, which hitherto he has not ventured openly to make, though he has for many years believed it to be a real truth; that is to say, that it opens figurative prophecy, like a master key, " *the key of knowledge*," and " *of David*."

He believes, that there will be, in the first place, *a merely spiritual advent of the Son of Man, in the spiritual clouds of the spiritual heaven*; of which advent, the doctrine of a universal analogy will be the vehicle, at least in part. *He believes*, that the time of this ad-

---

* Though the writer ventures to think it probable, that this *advent* may be, in some measure, personal and visible, yet he cannot imagine to himself any cause, that can induce a necessity for a *personal, visible, human, reign upon earth, during a thousand years, of our Lord Jesus Christ*. And as every such passage is *necessarily ambiguous*, so he must receive that sense which seems most reasonable to him.

vent is not far off, and to himself it has already taken place. It is plain that this advent is by the medium of *faith*, and therefore many will not believe it; indeed, it may well be said, under this view of the subject, " *when the Son* " *of Man cometh, shall he find faith on the* " *earth ?*"

In the seventeenth chapter of St. Luke, our Lord also says, " *For as the lightning that* " *lighteneth out of the one part under heaven,* " *shineth unto the other part under heaven; so* " *shall also the Son of Man be in His day.* BUT " FIRST MUST HE SUFFER MANY THINGS AND BE " REJECTED OF THIS GENERATION. *And as it* " *was in the days of Noe, so shall it be also in* " *the days of the Son of Man. They did eat,* " *they drank, they married wives, they were* " *given in marriage, until the day that Noe* " *entered into the ark, and the flood came and* " *destroyed them all,*" &c.*

Now, it appears to this writer, that both of the advents are described in the above Scripture. The first is an *incognito*, as it were, to those who have not faith, and not an open revelation; and this is figuratively implied by a

---

* It is a remarkable text in the fifteenth chapter of Revelations, that " *The temple of the tabernacle,* of the " *testimony in heaven,* was *opened;* and *no man was able to* " *enter into it, until* the seven plagues of the seven angels " were fulfilled."

coming in *clouds;* the clouds of *heaven,* not of the *earth.* The second advent is an *open revelation,* manifest to all, like the *lightning's flash.* It may, no doubt, be plausibly said, that the expression " *this generation,"* must mean the Jews who crucified our Lord ; but I believe it means the " *generation of vipers,"* as St. John Baptist calls the *Pharisees,* and *Sadducees,* or in other words, the *hypocrites* and *infidels* of all ages*.

Moreover, the progress of the dispensation of truth, during *the spiritual* or *cloudy advent,* until the arrival of the period of the *bright unclouded advent of open revelation,* is compared to the dispensation of the days of Noe. The patriarch builded his ark, preaching righteousness and repentance, during the term of one hundred and twenty years. Then came the flood, and destroyed all who had not entered the ark. The flood answers to the second advent of open revelation in flaming fire. The prophecy ends by saying, " *Even thus shall it be* " *in the day when the Son of Man is revealed."*

---

* The word *generation* does not always mean a literal race of men in Holy Scripture. Thus in Genesis, vi. it is said, " *These are the generations of Noah : Noah was a* " *just man, and perfect in his generations, and Noah walked* " *with God."* These are generations of spirit ; for we know that his generations after the flesh were not perfect, viz. Ham, the accursed.

It seems to be generally supposed, that our Lord meant to intimate in the eighteenth chapter of St. Luke, where he says, " *When* " *the Son of Man cometh, shall he find faith on* " *the earth?*" that at His coming openly to judgement, He should find very few, either nations or individuals, who would openly profess Christianity as a faith, or religion. But a more careful examination of the subject of the context will show, that He is there speaking of " *God's own elect, who cry* " *unto Him, day and night,*" and not of any open infidels, or of the world at large, except generally; for there could be no doubt about them; because He says, " *and shall not God* " *avenge* His *own elect, &c.?* *I tell you* HE " *will avenge them speedily.* NEVERTHELESS, " *when the Son of Man cometh, shall He find* " *faith on the earth?*" He cometh (as it appears) to deliver and avenge his own elect. But when he cometh, even *they* will not believe (at least for a while) that it is He. " *The* " *temple of the tabernacle of the testimony* " *in* HEAVEN* *is opened,*" as it were, to

---

* If there be an universal analogy between spiritual and natural things, then the spiritual heaven is contained. in the Word of God, and especially the New Testament. But *the earthly tabernacle* of *the spiritual temple* of heaven is the *natural visible creation,* in the same manner as *the body* of man is the *tabernacle of his spirit.* See 2 Cor. v. Also,

speak figuratively, as *an ark;* but they cannot enter into it, *until* certain caustic plagues have

Hebrews, viii. and ix. From all which it appears by the interpretations of analogy, that natural things of the visible creation, form an earthly tabernacle, which contains, in types or figures, a similitude of the testimony, which is hid in the mysteries of the spiritual heaven; which mysteries are opened, when it pleaseth the Lord, by the medium of a universal analogy, or by immediate inspiration, as in the Prophets.

ANALOGIC PARALLELS.

1. The natural, or symbolical, or typical heavens, or solar system, and stars; including *our atmosphere*, as a kind of common ground, or point of union between our heaven and earth.

1. Of the spiritual heavens, which contain the spiritual world; also, the written Word of God, which contains heaven, earth, sea, and the lower regions, in words full of " spirit and life," viz. *The Law*, and the *Gospel; Moses*, and *Jesus Christ; the moon*, and *the sun;* the light of *right reason*, and the light of *divine revelation;* the light of *nature*, or of *the earth ; the greater light to rule the day* and *the lesser light to rule the night of spiritual ignorance;* also *the stars* of light, or *preachers* and *prophecyers.* Also in a lower and subordinate degree, the rational intellect or spirit of man, *as an atmosphere*, and common point of union between men and pure spirits.

Supposed to be types

burnt away the *callous* of the evil heart of un-belief. *Therefore there must be some kind of disguise in His coming, as a trial of their faith,* and also as a corroborator of it by a gradual developement.

If there is any foundation of truth in the foregoing observations, then all who think so will see, that the doctrine of an universal analogy, between the visible and invisible things of God, may be most important to all men, and very edifying and consolatory to those who believe and understand it.

But I anticipate, that many if not all my readers, will here put the following searching questions to me: viz. What good has analogy done to *you?* or what benefit have *you* derived from it, beyond the mere notion (whether true or false) that it is the key of knowledge? Has it made *you* a more humble conscientious be-

| 2. The natural, or symbolical, or typical earth with its animals, waters, and its *atmosphere*, as a common point of connection with its heaven. | Supposed to be types of | 2. The moral earth, or the body of man, with all its members, appetites, and affections; also his *rational intellect*, as the highest part of man, and the lowest part of that polluted *heaven*, in which, by nature, reigns " *the prince of the power of the* " *air, the spirit that now worketh* " *in the children of disobedience."* |

3

liever? Has it increased and strengthened *your* practical faith, in making you a more pains-taking, hard-working labourer in the vineyard of Christ? He has taught us to judge of the tree by its fruits. What good fruits have *you* to show? " Thou that teachest another (by ana-
" logy), teachest thou not *thyself?*"

In reply to these questions, I must own that I cannot say much for myself; but much for analogy I *can* say. The study and belief of universal analogy, as it could only be received *by faith*, so it has increased and strengthened that hospitable principle, which opened the doors of the heart to entertain it. When the world, the flesh, and the devil united, have " *thrust sore at me, that I might fall,*—Psalm cxviii. often has the faith which springs from the view of analogy been an instrument of a good Providence, to keep me from falling away openly and finally. Often has it excited de-votional feelings of the most ardent kind, full of faith, hope, and love. Often has it made worldly pleasures and pursuits to appear like dung, in comparison of the faith and know-ledge of Christ Jesus my Lord. Often, or ra-ther continually, has it shown me that prayer is the golden pipe, the conductor of my vital air, my breath of life, and my soul's meat and drink. Often has it made me long for the

Q

coming and kingdom of our Lord Jesus Christ, whether spiritual or visible, figurative or literal ; and in proportion as the world, the flesh, and the devil, have succeeded in making me fear that universal analogy is a dream; or *rather* that it was dreaming to believe that the world would ever receive it, or derive any benefit from it; in the same ratio, my faith, hope, and love have gradually melted away, and almost vanished like the smoke of an expiring flame.

But I thank God, through Jesus Christ our Lord, that though I have passed through a long, dark, cold night, and winter of doubt, unbelief, fear, and aversion from the sun of righteousness; and defiled by the mire of sin, " *when the iniquity of my heels*" or my irregular moral walk) " *has*" (with dirt) " *compassed me* " *about*,"—Psalm xlix.; yet the spring-time of the promise, of a cheerful hope, appears again; and I feel a degree of spiritual renovation, in the faith and hope of my return to the sun of my soul, in the equinox of my spiritual orbit.

With respect to my good works, I confess that I have none to show; and if I *had*, I hope I should not think them worthy to be mentioned. But that (alas!) is my own fault, and not the fault of universal analogy, which has constantly taught me better things. So also has my Bible, its foundation; and if I perish (which God in mercy avert!) they both remain righteous, holy, and blameless! My blood must rest on my own head! Yet I still hope in God, through Jesus Christ our Lord. Amen.

THE END.

NOTE on PAGE 172, LINE 2.

* As a stick which is crooked, must, in order to be made straight, be bent the opposite way beyond the true straight line, so it is in religion and morality. The true straight line is this, " thou shalt love thy neighbour as " thyself." But this is not enough for fallen man; he re- quires more, viz. " *I say unto you, that ye resist not evil; but* " *whosoever shall smite thee on the right cheek, turn to him the* " *other also.*"

Printed by S. Gosnell, Little Queen Street, London.

LaVergne, TN USA
04 May 2010
181500LV00003B/127/P